THE
DISCERNING GENTI...
How to Survive the 100 Years War

People to Meet and Places to Plunder

With a foreword by Christopher Columbus's dad

By Lee Rotherham

www.BretwaldaBooks.com
@Bretwaldabooks
bretwaldabooks.blogspot.co.uk/
Bretwalda Books on Facebook
First Published 2015

Bretwalda Books
Unit 8, Fir Tree Close, Epsom, Surrey KT17 3LD
info@BretwaldaBooks.com
www.BretwaldaBooks.com

ISBN 978-1-909698-80-2

Printed and bound in Great Britain by Marston Book Services Ltd, Oxfordshire

Contents

Foreword

Europe for many years now has been a bit of a backwater. What with barbarians pulling down the Roman Empire, Vikings spoiling sea side holiday resorts, and Dark Age warlords hoofing around the countryside, most of the continent has been right down the bottom of the list for all but the most determined and rugged of backpackers.

Happily those times are beginning to change. Welcome to the latter part of the Middle Ages!

Latterly, the more regular tourist jaunts are increasingly past their prime. Constantinople, that gem on the cusp of the continent, has never recovered from being wrecked by the Fourth Crusade and for a time lost to a separate 'Latin' Empire. Rome is but a shadow of its former self, and while its ruins evoke ancient majesties they support a much faded small town and almost rural community – even the popes went away. Further afield, the Timurids are yet to overrun central Asia and Persia; Marco Polo's old China loiters under Mongol rule awaiting the Mings; Mameluke Cairo is set to sink into decline. So now truly is the time to put on your hiking shoes and explore somewhere new.

The area featuring in the Hundred Years War provides travellers with a myriad of opportunities. For merchants, the slow growth of urban life (plagues and pestilence apart) provide you with a chance to explore major and ancient trading routes, in a time of big budget spending on the artefacts of war. Soldiers of fortune, and even of principle, can join in on a cause and make a mint, or even better, rob one. Raiding and plundering in France can be extraordinarily profitable, and even in slack periods there's room for employment in garrisons and the chance to earn a regular wage.

But for true tourists and students of the modern world, wandering the battlefields of the Hundred Years War provides visitors with a rare opportunity to meet some extraordinary people - some heroes, some saints, some truly wicked and depraved. The scenery is fantastic; the architecture ambitious; the sanitation appalling but you can't have everything.

So pack your bags, gird your loins, and put on a scallop (we'll tell you about those later). You're coming with us on an adventure of a lifetime. Hopefully you might even survive it.

Gary Columbus

Chapter 1

An Introduction for Mediaeval Tourists

We appreciate that different people have different motives for coming on holiday to the Hundred Years War. Some people like to dress up in period armour and take part in battlefield enactments, to sense the whiff of gunpowder, or more likely, a neighbour's troubled pants in the middle of a hail of arrows. Some prefer to look at the imposing châteaux rather than camp outside one for six weeks during a tedious siege. Others are more interested in meeting famous people, preferably crazed as they are more entertaining.

Whatever your preferences, you need to have a basic understanding first of where you're at, to get the most out of your visit.

Britain and France in the early 14th Century

The first thing to note is that the action kicks off in 1337, and that it covers two main geographical areas. There's the island of Britain, and the territorial bloc known as France.

Britain is a large island off the coast of continental Europe. As anyone who has read their Latin authors knows, which is very few of us, it stretches out into the cold Atlantic. Far off lie the desolate lands discovered by the Vikings, but otherwise the ocean lies empty and void.

The main portion of the island is called England, occupied by a people known as the English. In the ancient past they formed separate kingdoms, but these have long united. To their west there are the Welsh peoples, descended from the Britons who occupied the island in Roman times. These have mostly, but not entirely, been subdued. To the north is a separate kingdom that has only recently won its independence again. This is called Scotland. It too is gradually creating a sense of unity, though ancient divisions still run deep.

Beyond the Welsh shore lies another large island known as Ireland or Hibernia. While culturally unique and therefore of interest, it does not feature prominently in the course of our studies.

In contrast, the ancient territory of Gaul, or France as it is today known, is politically far more divided. The division of power pits the central monarchy against great lords, jealous of their independence and in some cases with strong historical claims for a separate territory of their own.

Identity is fractured. There is no common language. In the north there is Picard French. Normandy has its own version, exported centuries ago with William the Conqueror over to England. Brittany has a Celtic language hearkening back to the confused movements of peoples at the close of the Roman Empire, and neighbouring it is a version fused with French. The south meanwhile sees the north as a land apart. It speaks Provençal, a totally different Romance language that has developed from the decay of Latin. In the south west is Gascon, another dialect besides. The Pyrenean borderlands find Basque and Catalan speakers too. Even the "French" dialects are markedly different from the language spoken around Paris and the French court.

Meanwhile, some of these territories have great dukes with histories of doing things their own ways. Brittany has a track record of being independent. Burgundy centuries ago used to be an independent kingdom. Parts of the francophone east still today lie within the territories of the neighbouring Holy Roman Empire. The south west of France, in olden times known as Aquitaine, is owned by the King of England – properly speaking these days he just runs Gascony and his borders and jurisdiction are a right muddle. Meanwhile, with roads being as bad as they are and transport difficult, local rulers can get quite used to simply running things the way they want to.

If you think it's difficult governing a country that makes a thousand different cheeses, think what it must be like trying to rule such a fractious polyglot land. So while France has a huge head start in any squaring off with its island neighbour thanks to being much bigger and more populated, it's far from a united country. That will be hugely important in the years ahead.

Why the scrapping?

So just why is there all this fighting between England and France? It must be a fairly hefty argument if it's going on for so long?

In fact, the origins go back a long, long way.

Three hundred years ago, England was anglo-saxon and quite a different place. We tend to think of it these days as a bit backward, but it was tremendously well run, rich, had wonderful large old abbeys reaching up into the sky, with marvellous craft industries, evocative poetry, and beards to boot. But for reasons we won't go into here, along came the Normans and they conquered the place.

The effect was devastating culturally. The place became normanised. Within a handful of years of the Conquest, even the number one boy's name was William.

Anglo-Saxon was the language of the conquered, Norman French the language of the court. It's a status we'll see continuing to this day (though watch it change as this war goes on).

It also embroiled England into the politics of the continent in a way it had previously been spared. The nation had traded with its neighbours. It had even gone in for some dynastic marriages with nobility on the other side of the water. Exiled members of the royal family had certainly done the European rounds. But the historic links had often been to Scandinavia thanks to the old Viking links, and they hadn't involved major military expeditions.

Now though there was a Norman dynasty on the throne in England. That meant the prospect of land wars on the continent with Normandy's neighbours. It also meant complicating an already fraught legal nicety.

The Duke of Normandy did not properly speaking own his lands across the Channel. The Normans had been granted them a century and a half ago, allowing them to settle on French territory to stop them from seasonal pillaging from Scandinavia. But in return they accepted they had a boss in the shape of the King of France. Whatever ambiguities on how independent they were meant to be had been settled as French royal power grew, and it was quite clear that the Dukes were vassals of the French Crown. Yet with the conquest of England, the Normans suddenly became monarchs in their own right. Thus William and his heirs were simultaneously equal in status to the French King with their new territories, but junior in their old.

So a marvellous way to wind up the Normans was to require them to come and abase themselves before the new French king as all good vassals should. If they didn't turn up, well that was treason so you could go to war and grab their land. Thus, three centuries of psychological poking with a pointy stick accounts for part of the problems today.

This isn't the whole story though. A lucky marriage gave the Kings of England a huge slice of south west France. A disastrous war then lost it. They did keep a slight sliver of the south west coastline, including the important port of Bordeaux. They also kept their French language and psychology of being continental in outlook. They just didn't have anyone grabbing them by the sleeve and saying, "Leave it Harry, he's not worth it, get back inside the pub." So while they still had to demonstrate their fealty for Bordeaux, they still remembered they once used to own really large chunks of the rest of France and wanted it back.

The last war left a lot of Gascony in a right state. French territory sits in the middle of English lands, and vice versa. Local lords profit from the confused legal position by pushing their own private vendettas against their neighbours, and when the King-Duke tries to stop it, the aggressor has a tricky habit of appealing to the highest court in the land. That happens to be the parlement at Paris, not London. In the meantime the miscreant is immune, and a clever lord can keep the lawyers busy for years. When a decision does come back, more often than not the King of France's men support the claim that's more hostile to English interests.

Meanwhile, tensions between the two monarchs remain. Scotland, England's troublesome land neighbour, receives French support in its fight for independence. The French are playing politics in the Low Countries, crucial for England's trade, and they poke around in the internal politics of Gascony's barons.

A final key point though relates to the dynastic succession. For years the Kings of England and France have married into each other's families, along with those of other noble houses. However, something unusual happened in the early fourteenth century. For hundreds of years, succession has run according to the old system, meaning that the eldest son inherits his father's throne. But in 1316, the baby king Jean I died. This created a bit of a crisis, and it was decided to skip his child sister and jump to his uncle, Philip V. The real crisis, however, came after both he and his brother Charles IV then died. Charles too had a sister, Isabella, who this time was grown up and married to a magnate powerful enough to support her.

Unfortunately, that man also happened to be the King of England. This created a bit of a problem. That man, Edward III, pointed out that his wife and he had a son, and claimed that the inheritance should jump to him. As an extra complication, the first princess who had been passed over also by now had a male heir, the King of Navarre, who would become quite a sticky character.

Isabella though also had a male cousin via an uncle, who had the decided advantage for other people in the French court of not being foreign at all.

It was all rather complicated. The matter went to review, which seemed like a civilised outcome. The great nobles who made up the court ruled that Isabella couldn't transmit a right she herself didn't have; and that the real king was the cousin Philip VI. Edward took it on the chin, did his fealty on bended knee to the new King, and left it there.

That was then. This is now.

Armagnacs and Burgundians

They sound like things you'd stash away in a drinks cabinet. But those two names spell a package of trouble in the fifteenth century. It would pay you well to understand this bit before you start talking politics in a French tavern.

The struggle between the Kings of England and France we explained above gets complicated by even more strife. Once again, it's a family business.

Philip is a son of King Jean II of France. He marries well. Extremely well. He becomes ruler by marriage of a chunk of eastern France, and with it gets the title of Duke of Burgundy. He also rules a slice of the Low Countries, which have excellent trading relations with England thanks to the cloth trade. That link of itself is enough to create tensions with those in the French court who might want to block English exports.

His elder brother Charles V of France dies, leaving a child, also called Charles, as king. Burgundy is one of several key people during the Regency. In due course, Charles VI assumes power as an adult.

But Charles then has a funny turn. Burgundy seizes the opportunity provided by the king's madness to assume a dominant position and dominate the government.

Not everyone agrees though with that state of affairs. The King's own brother, Louis, and Burgundy jostle for control for several years, before the latter dies. But the jockeying for power within the royal court continues.

Louis had married the daughter of the count of Armagnac. That gave his side some tangible support, and a faction name. The friction mounts.

Within a couple of years, this has escalated to territorial power play, street manoeuvres, and finally, political assassination – first of Louis; then it's Philip's son and heir, John of Burgundy in 1419. What follow is out-and-out civil war. The Burgundians, at first equivocal, now back the English.

So you can tell the sides apart, the English have as their symbol a red cross of St George on a white background; the French king uses a white cross on blue (also their old crusading emblem) or a white cross on red; the supporters of the Dauphin, the French Crown Prince, wear dolphin badges; and the Duke of Burgundy has a red cross of St Antony (which is diagonal and looks thorny). The Scots have a diagonal white cross on a blue background, though you can better spot them by the smoke from burning buildings on the horizon when they invade. The French king also has an ancient personal standard known as the oriflamme, which keeps getting lost on battlefields these days.

The confused business will last until 1435, when the French King recognises that the Burgundians should not longer be treated as mere vassals. The English are swiftly deprived of a vital ally, and cannot afford alone to fight on or even support their garrisons. The writing is on the wall.

All the world's a stage...

But only certain sets are being used in this production. The key venues are all in France, which is where most of the fighting is taking place. You can break these down into four blocks.

First, there's the area running from Brittany to Normandy and up the coast towards Calais – the northern littoral, nudging into the Low Countries. These are the areas that fall back slowly into English sway, and Normandy in particular is a prize that the English become determined to hold onto. Then there's the northern hinterland, down to Paris, and the high water mark of the English conquests. Third, there's Aquitaine and the south west, to start with just a thin strip but growing back into the traditional territories anciently held. Finally, there's the Loire Valley, the fertile area and all the feeder rivers that includes Anjou and Touraine and the parade of increasingly fine castles.

There's more to see than just these areas though. There's excitement in northern Wales and some sticky battles on the Scottish front too. There's even French raiding of the south coast - duty free gone bad.

On top of the battlefields, there are a number of charming towns and cities worth a detour. For instance, London is such a hotchpotch of timber buildings it's a wonder there hasn't been a Great Fire since King John's time, or a second order one since Westminster went ablaze in 1299, so it might be worth visiting them while they are still in their current condition. There are a number of outstanding cathedrals, such as Salisbury's which is just seeing its tower and spire being completed, or the great windows going into York Minster. Then there are the great castles, such as Warwick which is being remodelled. As French raiders become a menace, several delightful castles appear in the south, such as Bodiam, and Scotney. New technologies and designs lead to wonderful changes in architecture, culminating in the lofty parapets of Tattershall castle made out of an emerging fabric – brick.

So even in quieter parts of the realm, there are wondrous things to see. Long gone are the days of austere Norman churches, sturdy towers and dull dwellings. Variety is the spice of life. Which is just as well, as spices are extremely rare and expensive imports.

Chapter 2
Planning Your Visit

Tourist Seasons

To help travellers plan their stay in the theatre of operations, we've broken down the period into three blocks. Each has its own quirks, styles, issues and advantages. Our timings are a little arbitrary but give a starting point for planning around.

The High Season runs from 1337 to 1369. This era is particularly well-suited for those who prefer the grand romance of large numbers of shiny knights doing heroic activity and having songs sung about them. A very marked down side, unfortunately, is the serious likelihood that tourists risk encountering bubonic plague during their sojourn. On the other hand, those staying away will ultimately find the problem coming to them a year or two earlier or later anyhow, so if you are going to drop dead in the street you may as well do it somewhere interesting.

Mid Season covers the period roughly running 1369 – 1415. This is quite a destructive period, so if romantic ruins are your thing then this is certainly a good moment to pick. The French maintain the upper hand through much of this period, so it might be advisable to concentrate more on English domestic settings. This is particularly advisable once an extremely angry short fellow called du Guesclin packs himself into armour and goes on a near-single-handed rampage through English lines.

On the other hand, the Low Season 1415 – 1453 has a very different appeal. You may less appreciate it if you are a French peasant. Taking advantage of splits in the French royal family, the English army goes on a spree, culminating in a treaty that – if honoured – delivers the whole country to Henry V once his French counterpart dies. But Hal dies too. Henry VI is not up to the task of looking after England, let alone managing two kingdoms, and Joan of Arc's appearance helps revitalise French morale. With Burgundy back on board, a reunited France proves too powerful for the English to resist, but even now great moments of drama and heroism play out.

Meanwhile, a scenario of social revolution, religious questioning, linguistic dynamism and scientific development, including in architecture, is playing out. All this, with a backdrop of royal courts, tourneys, exquisitely illustrated books and fine costumes. Or if you are travelling in steerage, wattle and daub plus mud.

Highlights

1   *The Burghers of Calais*
When England captures Calais, its dogged resistance spells doom for its defendants. Six brave locals resolve to take the penalty upon themselves. Watch this moment of pathos, as the Queen of England intercedes with her husband to spare their lives. It's a monumental introduction to the strong link between this fortress town and the island across the waters.

2   *The Maid of Orleans*
Some call her God's lieutenant to the French. Others say she's a crazed cross-dresser. You decide. Watch the court make up its mind whether to burn Joan at the stake (spoiler alert: Take some Rouen sausages with you).

3   *Black Death*
First you get big bumps. Then you get black blotches. Then you die. Welcome to the world of swift death and mass graves.

4   *St Crispin's Day*
It's a battle that pits a tired outnumbered force against an overwhelming army of knights. But glorious victory awaits the underdog. Watch the hour of glory for Henry V at Agincourt. Fotheringhay holds the tomb of one of the few English knights to fall that day, the brave Duke of York

5   The first Reformation

You may have lucked out on catching sight of the Cathars, but there are interesting times afoot. Witness the first reformation as the Lollards challenge the Catholic Church. Scripture takes centre stage over dogma, and that means the revolution of translating the bible into English. Rispeck to Wycliffe, man.

6   The birth of modern English

English is growing as the medium of the land, replacing court French. Meet the first of the great English writers in the vernacular, Geoffrey Chaucer, author of the celebrated Canterbury Tales.

7   The Last Prince of the Welsh

For centuries the Welsh have fought to keep their independence and identity faced with the English invader. Watch now the last gasp of ancient glory as a final native ruler arises as Prince of Wales, and comes within a short grasp of achieving his goal.

8   The glories of Rheims

The crowning capital of France – literally. All of the great houses of God have their divine artwork. But Rheims is the cathedral where French monarchs go to seek anointment and coronation. Witness the splendour, pageantry ... and political intrigue of a rush job.

9   Popular Revolts

History is about the ordinary people too. In England there's Wat Tyler and the Peasant's Revolt, plus Jack Cade's rebellion. Over in France there's the horror of the Jacquerie, and a persistent number of larger than life robbers, thieves, scallywags and desperadoes leading bands of ordinary people whom life has trampled on. It's time for them to get their own back, or die trying.

10   The end of the Middle Ages: 1453

They don't come more epoch-making than the ending of an epoch. The close of this period marks the dividing line between the mediaeval and the modern. Take the last opportunities time has to offer to wander in the final twilight of centuries of chivalry and semi-antiquity, before you become Renaissance Man. Two great battles in the east and west – Castillon, and the fall of Constantinople, put the full stop at the end of the book. Loiter on its last page for a short while longer.

Getting there

The Hundred Years War is no time to be travel sick.

One of the attractions for potential visitors is the relative ease by which travellers can arrive at their destination.

Ports are obviously central to anyone planning to travel beyond France and into England. Happily, there are a number of harbours on both sides of the Channel that offer opportunities for a crossing, particularly when on the French coast the harbour is held for England. The trip is relatively short but do plan your journey to avoid the more tempestuous winter crossings if you can avoid it. Sea travel even over such relatively short distances is not entirely safe. It has been a couple of centuries since the infamous White Ship Disaster killed the heir to the English Throne and naval designs have improved since then, but no vessel is unsinkable in a storm, especially the more top-heavy of the cogs. There's no need for blind fear though, since hundreds of merchants regularly make crossings from as far south as Bordeaux as part of the lucrative wine trade.

Harbours also provide an alternative to travelling by land between those towns perched on the same shore. Local transport can be available and might shave off some time, for instance when crossing the Bristol Channel, or hopping from Boston to Lincoln. But if on horseback and unencumbered by merchants' wares, you might find a direct ride quicker because of issues of wind direction and tide.

Roads

France is part of mainland Europe, and as such lies on the modern track network. It is true that these are not as grand as in ancient days when the Romans ran the place, as you can tell from those spots where traces of ancient paved and drained roadways still survive. Nevertheless, the existence of a number of bridges – and where the river is too wide and deep, ferries – means that travelling between towns is a relatively painless affair. Bandits permitting, of course.

When planning your trip, bear in mind that weather will affect these routes, particularly if you are using wheeled transport like carts. Typically, they are little maintained, unless near wealthy abbeys or close to the estates of nobility with a personal property interest. Coming across better quality tracks is a good sign you may be near somewhere where you might shelter for the night, and if you find yourself on cobblestones you're already in a well-to-do conurbation. Where conditions are bad though, do take care as cases of people having accidents on lanes are recorded.

Even in wealthy and important households, you may often see two people riding the same horse, or using a mule. So we suggest applying a universal level of courtesy to all fellow road users rather than ribaldry: you never know whom you might be mocking.

Travellers moving individually or in very small parties on official business might consider seeking approval to use what may exist locally of the network of rested horses. These are intended to allow couriers to travel speedily to court, which travels around the land listening to local grievances. You would have to be extremely well-connected tourists to be able to use them, but if in a hurry such permission could knock days off your travel time.

When planning your journey, bear in mind that rather than camping out in cold or wet weather, inns are often sited at convenient points in between settlements.

It's possible, particularly in poor weather, you might get lost. In pasture land do take care if you believe you've found the route again: you might have wandered onto a drovers' track designed to take livestock to market, or to and from seasonal pastures. Choose the wrong direction and you may in fact be heading away from civilisation rather than towards it. At certain times of year, on these tracks you might find yourself encountering drovers pushing on huge herds of all kinds of animals, from cattle to geese. Some patience may be required as these animals pass.

Pilgrims' routes on the other hand are those lanes that run from the main urban centres to places of religious importance. In England, there is a short road that runs to the shrine of Walsingham. A pilgrimage route runs through south Wales to St David's, though that's a little wilder in terms of scenery and lawlessness. Canterbury is another location that draws the crowds, and has even inspired a recent great piece of English writing. Scotland has St Andrew's.

Parts of England's south coast running to the ports also carry traces of pilgrims' walks. That's because of the routes on the French side, which run in two main directions. The first is to Rome, the headquarters of the Church. The second is to the shrine of St James, in Santiago de Compostela in North West Spain.

In England, all roads lead to London – or the five major ones do anyway. The first great route runs from London to Cornwall. The second, to Bristol. The third, to Carlisle. The fourth, the Great North Road, stretches out through Yorkshire up to the Scottish border. The last runs over to South West Wales. There are, however, still a number that bisect these and cut across the radial network. The Roman routes and their ancient predecessors thus still survive even after all these centuries as basic free ways. Expect to be able to ride thirty miles on a good day, even more if you are in a hurry, but perhaps only a fifth of that if the weather is rotten. Obviously, travelling on foot after rains can be quite miserable.

Highwaymen can be an issue on some stretches at certain periods, particularly in France but also in parts of Britain as the wars drag to a close. Do remember that highways are protected by the King's Peace, meaning that crime should be reported to local agents of the Crown for them to act on. If you are lucky, it's possible you might be able to retrieve robbed goods with the help of the local Sheriff, or at least see the satisfaction some weeks later of seeing the villains (and villeins) strung up.

We highly recommend carrying caltrops, iron spikes that can be thrown on the ground to deter pursuit. These days even assassins of princes use them in Paris when they make their getaways.

Weather

Our area of interest stretches from the Pyrenees and the vineyards of the South of France, to the bleak hills of the intemperate north. You will need to pack a variety of clothing depending on which region you'll be visiting. Good boots are advised, particularly in the hillier north and west of Britain.

Note that it rains a lot in England. If you don't have anything waterproof, bring a second set of clothing.

Some commentators suggest that the climate has been improving of late, but that in the fifteenth century we can anticipate a dip in temperatures again. If so, you can always buy something made out of quality English wool during your visit to keep the chills away.

The Great Drowning

A huge sou'westerly gale strikes Britain and the Low Countries in January 1362. It will drag down the spire of Norwich's cathedral, rip over trees, and complete the work done by earlier storms in creating the inner sea off Holland, the Zuider Zee. Coastal communities are engulfed and lost.

Stay in port and ideally on high ground. Thousands will die. Also be alert for other disastrous storms in 1421 and 1446. Learn to swim.

The Region in Outline

Geography

France consists mainly of rolling low hills and flat plains, particularly in the north and west. The south is warmer, and around the Massif Central area is more mountainous and less verdant. There are large numbers of rivers, of which the principle are the Loire, the Rhone, the Seine, the Garonne/Dordogne confluence, and cutting across the Flemish territories the mouth of the Rhine. They provide for a largely well-watered and rich agricultural land. There are many ports and harbours. Crops vary according to the climate and soil.

Britain is similar in many ways to France's north, though it is slightly less temperate. The north and west are more rugged. The coast hosts a number of celebrated fishing towns that provide quality exports, particularly of herring. A key feature of the landscape is the presence of sheep farming in large numbers, both for wool export and increasingly to support a domestic cloth trade.

Huge tracks of land remain forested. However, perhaps it's the Black Death reducing policing, perhaps in some areas it's through an increased need for timber for buildings or mine workings, but revisit an area a few years later and you might start to spot the amount of wooded area literally being cut back.

That said, many forests aren't simply patches of land for rambling and squirrel spotting. A large number are crown estate. Under no circumstances get caught hunting in these, because that's poaching and if caught the penalties are extremely serious indeed.

Urban conurbations are small, with even the largest cities (that is to say, towns with a bishop) holding no more than a few thousand residents at most. While we haven't stopped to count everyone, at a guess we'd say the population of London is perhaps one twentieth the size of a great world city like Cairo at this time.

The peoples

The territories you will be visiting are far from culturally and ethnically uniform. That's why you'll find people with all manner of strange and wonderful names, like Perkin, Kouk, Pregent, Fulk, Tuddual, Guillonet, Franquet or Bando.

The English in the Low Season do not have a good reputation. True, other countries marvel at their accelerating martial prowess, and the way they have swiftly changed from being backwards military ragamuffins. But they have the reputation of being haughty, swift to anger, and slow to cool down. They like fighting and are greedy; they are unfriendly as diplomats, suspicious, cheating and proud. The middle classes are untrustworthy, the ordinary people cruel and disloyal. Only their nobles are loyal and upright, but they know their people well and pay for their support and employment. Most shocking of all, the representatives of the fickle crowd often refuse to pay taxes when the King asks.

Britain remains divided by the aftermath of invasions. The majority of ordinary people in England are English speakers. The accent varies considerably, and you'll find plenty of wonderful variations in local words that show a slang dating back to Saxon differences. You may come across hints of old Viking links with some of the place names for example. But the real difference lies with the French language, since the top class still use the language of the Conquest.

A different invasion era marks out the people of the west. Notwithstanding English dominion, the Welsh continue to retain a separate identity, along with their language. With its last free state having lost its independence in the thirteenth century, the famed Welsh archers of the north and spearmen of the south have become a solid feature of English armies. The early fifteenth century sees its last flowering as an independent state briefly re-emerges.

Wales's lot remains an improvement on the fate of the West Welsh, or Cornish. This county is now the domain of the King's heir, the Black Prince. While it retains a unique identity, self-governed through Stannary parliaments and mining courts, its language and Welshness have by now been heavily subsumed.

Scotland's identity is a separate tale again. It has had more success than the Welsh in fighting off the Normans and their heirs, and has lately become fully independent once more. Ironically, culturally its ruling class shares French tastes with its English opponents, defining its rulers just as much as in England in opposition to the man on the street (or rather, track). So if you are a whizz at French, do display it when visiting high society. On the other hand, English will do you just fine in the town in the south. Out in the highlands and islands, Gaelic is spoken. The chances are though that unless you are looking to hire some gallowglass mercenaries carrying unfeasibly huge swords, or pushing the limits for your export markets, you won't need to travel to such distant and inhospitable parts. This is a shame as while the amenities are truly basic, the scenery is spectacular and the nightlife quite wild.

If anything, the situation in France is even more diverse. Some parts may seem a little familiar. In the western peninsular, you have the wonderful Breton culture, which is an invigorated Welsh nation making full use of a preponderance of cider. The legends of King Arthur live on in Paimpont Forest, locally equated to Brocéliande, the forest reputed to hide Merlin and home of a rock with the power to summon storms (we tried it and it did rain, though to be fair it was already overcast). The peninsular also provides much bounty for lovers of seafood. A Celtic language is spoken here: it's said if you put a native in the same room as a Welshman, a Cornishman, an Irishman and a Gael from Scotland, they will just about be able to understand one another. A fight over whether to drink whisky or cider might then ensue.

It's the Count that counts

With roads being what they are, central authority decreases the further away you are from the royal court. That helps to explain why kings have long had a tendency of roaming the countryside looking for issues to resolve, and why monarchs have castles and homes dotted around their lands. Don't think of dropping by one to visit when they're out though: they take their furniture and tapestries with you, so you'll have a pretty basic stay.

In any event, it would be a mistake to believe where you have a problem that you have set off to see the monarch, or hang around for months waiting for him to drop by the area. The solution may well be local.

Travellers who have issues that need resolving, such as merchants who have a problem with terms of a contract, can often use local magistrates or nobles.

In England, it's important to recognise that power is becoming comparatively less central. It's a slow process, but increasingly it's not who you are, but the job you have, that makes you an important figure locally. That's certainly true the more towns get charters from the King and become self-

Some barons will have the shirt off your back.

governing. Meanwhile, courts and legal process have developed from the principles underpinning the Magna Carta and are placing more emphasis on professionals interpreting and arguing the law, rather than judgements by rich people sitting at a high table in their castle.

That's not to say that the legal process hasn't advanced in France. Paris has a strong reputation as a centre of excellence. But out in the regions, it's probably fair to say that various dukes and counts have a much greater importance since they are less prepared to accept higher authority, and may be more prepared to bend the rules, at least until the French King convincingly wins the war at any rate. It rather depends on whether you're in an area that he holds in his own right and thus has direct control over – typically those parts of France his ancestors conquered, like Normandy, or gained by marriage.

The key point for voyagers to note is that there are different powers at play in the places they visit. In free towns, it would be wise to keep in with the rich burghers, the guilds, and people holding administrative office. Other towns will fall under the sway of the resident bishop, or perhaps a powerful nobleman. It may be worthwhile checking out before you visit a tourist destination just who is really in charge of things locally, so you know whose servants not to offend in the tavern.

Making Preparations

What to Bring

France and England are modern, civilised countries where the majority of items you may need can be purchased locally. We recommend a small bag for day trips out into the country, and possibly a crossbow.

Hundred Years War battlefields are not very safe areas. If you are taking part in them as a combatant, we recommend you bring your full ironmongery paraphernalia, and some friends. Even as a merchant there are many areas where robbery and murder is a real threat, so travel in groups or with an escort. In some areas you might also be suspected if you don't carry arms, but do bear in mind that within cities, particularly during periods of cease fire, openly carrying them may bring you a visit from the town guard.

Hats are a good idea if you intend to do any besieging in summer.

If you are planning on doing any hiking, wear sturdy boots and keep to the tracks, which may also be the main road and therefore unlikely to be frequented by bears. Outdoors camping is considered acceptable, though frowned upon in cities except for lepers. A tent in urban environments would in any circumstances be considered going too far.

Prelude
Nothing happens in isolation. Here are the key events
leading to the Hundred Years War

War of Saint-Sardes. 1324 French move in to protect the rights of a French abbey, whose offshoot is in Gascon territory. French conquer most of the duchy.

Usurpation of kings. 1327 murder of Edward II. A regency in England involving the Queen Mother and Mortimer. 1330 coup by young prince, Edward III. Mortimer executed.

The Saintes War. 1330 French move in again. Saintes taken. Ceasefire. Recent conquests returned to Edward III but not old losses.

Second War of Scottish Independence. 1326 Treaty of alliance between Scotland and France. 1328 Treaty of Northampton recognises Scottish independence. 1332 pro-English Edward Balliol and Scots exiles invade to regain their lost lands. Win **(b) Dupplin Moor.** French alliance broken. But then driven out. 1333 first of several English invasions to secure promised southern castles. **(b) Halidon,** Berwick annexed by English. 1334 David II in exile in France. Arrives just in time to scupper Anglo-French peace talks. Scottish insurgency. 1335 large scale English invasion. 1336 Aberdeen destroyed to prevent a French force from landing.

Rising French tensions, 1334-1337. 1334 another dispute over Gascon land. Edward III refuses to accept a legal ruling. 1336 French raid southern England. Invasion scare. Paris parlement orders surrender of town of Puymirol. Edward III refuses. Philip VI uses excuse of political asylum granted by English to exile Robert of Artois to trigger war. 1337 Rhine princes already outraged by French buying up strategic towns look to Edward for support: the alliance shifts attention to northern France. The Emperor sells his support to Edward.

	High Season 1337 - 1369	
	The start of the war offers some of the more chivalrous moments, before the pillaging and murder swiftly become routine and tit-for-tat, and large parts of the countryside fall under the sway of former mercenaries turned brigands. But there are some real glory events too.	
King of England	**Events**	**King of France**
Edward III **1327 - 1377**	**Outbreak of war**, 1337-1340. 1337+, see-saw fighting in Aquitaine. French naval blockade. 1338 Portsmouth sacked, Guernsey captured, Jersey raided by French. English wool embargo in Flanders successfully triggers regime change and armed neutrality. Official start of the 100 Years War as Edward III renounces French suzerainty and finally, in the midst of a financial crisis, crosses the Channel with an army to join up with the German princes, who are now wavering. Massive bribery at the Imperial court, but all with borrowed money. Meanwhile, the French start to debase their currency. In the south, a French attempt to seize Penne by bribery fails hugely expensively when the commander leaves with the money but the garrison retires to the citadel, forcing the French to split their forces. 1339 Harwich menaced. Jersey castle withstands a siege. English convoy bumps into a French fleet, pushing it into harbour at Sluys. English victory, but neutrals caught up too. French raid Plymouth but have to withdraw. Burn Hastings, wreck Rye. But Genoese ships mutiny over pay not being passed on to them; French navy greatly weakened and returning sailors back an anti-French coup at home too. French fail narrowly to take Bordeaux. English raid French coast, Flemish sack Dieppe. Edward invades northern France. Battle nearly happens at Buirenfosse but neither side starts. English withdraw. 1340 Anglo-Flemish alliance. Edward claims the French crown, which covers the latter's defection legally as he technically becomes their overlord as French monarch. English raid Boulogne, destroying a fleet but with cost. March on Tournai but Earls of Salisbury and Norfolk are captured on a recce of Lille: their leaderless	**Philip VI** **1328-1350**

Edward III **1327 - 1377**	army disbands. French push into Hainault, but are surprised and routed at Valenciennes. French invasion fleet set for England arrives in the Low Countries. (b) Sluys (again): the aggressive English smash through the French shipping lines and take most of the vessels. (b) St Omer: confusion leads to Anglo-Flemish retreat. Tournai finally near to falling, but allies again wobbly. Truce agreed based on current positions. Edward dashes for England to escape his creditors.	**Philip VI** **1328-1350**

The return of the Scottish king. 1341 Scots capture Edinburgh. David II returns. 1342 raid into Northumberland. Capture of Sterling and Roxburgh.

The Breton inheritance. 1341 death of Jean III, Duke of Brittany. Jean de Montfort and Jeanne Penthièvre/Charles de Blois dispute the succession. The French back the latter, pushing the former into the English camp. He is defeated and taken before English help arrives. His wife though fights on vigorously. English support trickles through, while fighting escalates on Aquitaine's borders. 1342 French sack Southampton. 1343 truce based on current holdings. 1344 loss of Quimper to pro-French: executions. Most of anti-French party give up and English hold a few points only. 1345 Jean de Montfort escapes to fight again in Brittany, but dies. His son, another Jean, succeeds though but a child.

Escalation into general war. 1345 freelancing free for all vs French in south west. Bergerac captured. Scots raid (more to follow). (b) Auberoche: French attempt to break a siege is badly defeated. 1346 banking crisis as debts fail to be settled.

The sweep across northern France. 1346, Edward III lands on the Cherbourg peninsular. St Lô amongst many towns captured, inhabitants not spared. Caen city captured. Much of north west plundered. Meanwhile, Anglo-Flemish forces move south. (b) Crécy. Philip VI tries to cut off the English line of advance but is cut to pieces instead. Edward

Edward III **1327 - 1377**	is left free rein to advance along the coast. Realising he is not strong enough to conquer vast tracts, he besieges Calais as a permanent advance base. In the south, Poitiers captured. (b) Neville's Cross. Scots mauled, David II captured. In Calais, 'useless mouths' expelled from town but starve between the lines. Calais surrenders; lives spared but city confiscated. Truce agreed, which proves wobbly.	**Philip VI** **1328-1350**
	The Black Death. 1348 reaches southern France and spreads like wildfire. Multiple waves resurface after winter. Even more fatal respiratory second waves follow the first. Half of Paris dies. Parts of Gascony and some English villages see death rates of two in three. Several more outbreaks will follow over the century.	
	Resumption of general war. 1349 Major English strike into Languedoc as peace becomes notional on all French fronts. 1350 attempt to bribe a Calais captain backfires on the French. Advance guard admitted then captured: the captain is allowed to go on holiday by his boss, but later captured and dismembered. Philip VI remarries: friction with son. Philip VI dies. Jean II crowned, executes his Constable for trying to pay a ransom with key territory. 1351 Combat of the Thirty in Brittany. English raid from Calais ends in defeat at (b) Ardres. Brittany campaign expands to lower Loire. Truce, ignored in the south. 1352 Classic freebooting: Guines captured by a Englishman, John Dancaster, who's recruited some people on the Calais street and decides to give it a whirl. (b) Mauron, pro-French Bretons mauled. North of Aquitaine retaken by English.	
	Murder most horrid. 1354, Constable of France murdered in an inn by the household of the King of Navarre, who for now joins the English cause. An English army is prepped but Navarre and Jean II are reconciled. Peace terms. An Anglo-French peace treaty is signed, with Edward to drop the claim on the throne in exchange for the ancient Aquitaine territories, the	**John II** **1350 – 1364**

Edward III **1327 - 1377**	Loire provinces, and Calais. Pending news of this to spread, (b) Montmuran, English defeat in Brittany. Huge ransom agreement reached over David II, but Scots war preparations forestall his release. French court backtracks on confirming treaty. Jean II moves against Charles of Navarre's lands; Charles seeks English help.	**John II** **1350 – 1364**
	The rise of the Black Prince. 1355 Prince Edward raids Languedoc, 1356 Loire. **(b) Poitiers**: French disaster, Jean II and many nobles captured. Truce. 1357 Jean II taken to England. Power struggle in Paris.	
	Mob rule 1357, Regent forced to sign the Grand Ordinance, a sort of French Magna Carta. However, it is never implemented. Political strife escalates. **The Jacquerie:** 1358, local murders turn into a huge peasants' revolt in France. Peasants try to take royal residence but beaten off thanks to heroism by the Count of Foix and the Captal de Buch, cousins back from a crusade and on opposite sides in the War. Class war ruthlessly put down with much bloodshed.	
	A time of settlement. Treaty of London, 1359. Jean II concedes Greater Aquitaine to the English along with an astronomical ransom. The ransom doesn't arrive so the Loire provinces are added. Paris rejects the terms. Edward III marches on Rheims to crown himself King of France there, but cannot take it. 1360, French pillage Winchelsea, Rye. Edward plunders Burgundy and the outskirts of Paris. **Treaty of Brétigny:** ransom reduced considerably, Edward to surrender claim on the French throne, keep Calais, gain south west France. Deal agreed as Treaty of Calais. **1363 Truce of Evran:** Brittany to be split between the two claimants.	
	The Great Drowning. 1362, huge and terrible storm kills tens of thousands.	
	Settlement betrayed. 1362, Duke of Anjou breaks parole, ransom payments behind, French court	

King of England	Events	King of France
Edward III **1327 - 1377**	refuses to honour the treaty. Jean II keeps to his word and returns to English captivity, where he dies.	**John II** **1350 – 1364**
	Brittany settled. Lawlessness rife across France. 1364 **(b) Auray:** pro-French claimant to Brittany killed. 1365, **Treaty of Guérande,** pro-English claimant to become Duke but as a French vassal.	
	Spanish War. 1365, du Guesclin leads an offloaded army of unemployed mercenaries, now brigands, on a crusade in Spain. They opt to provoke a revolt in Castile instead. They back the usurper Enrique/ Henry II; Prince Edward and King of Navarre support Pedro/Peter the Cruel. Anglo-Gascon freebooters allowed to withdraw home. Navarre bribed but switches sides yet again. 1367, **(b) Najera:** Enrique's forces smashed. But King Pedro does not pay the English his debts, ruining their finances. 1368, Black Prince summoned to Paris: he threatens to take an army with him. John II resolves to back Enrique to undermine the English there.	**Charles V** **1364 – 1380** **Regent**

Mid Season 1369- 1415	
:---:	
France might be in a mess, but over this period we see English fortunes wane.	

King of England	Events	King of France
Edward III **1327 - 1377**	**The French fight back begins.** 1369, Charles V sends du Guesclin back to Spain. **(b) Montiel**, Pedro defeated then killed: his claim passes to his eldest daughter who will subsequently marry John of Gaunt. French meanwhile repudiate peace treaty and declare war. English pillage Normandy and Picardy. 1370 Bishop of Limoges bribed into defecting to French. Prince Edward ruthlessly destroys the city, gaining the moniker of Black Prince. Meanwhile, du Guesclin establishes his military reputation by beating a smaller English force at **(b) Pontvallain.** 1372 **(b)** La Rochelle, French naval victory allows them to retake Poitiers, and La Rochelle itself. 1373 John of Gaunt burns his way across France from	**Charles V** **1364 - 1380**

Edward III **1327 - 1377**	Calais to Bordeaux, but ruining his own army in the process. 1374 truce. **John Wycliffe.** 1370's rise to celebrity and friendship with John of Gaunt, Duke of Lancaster. 1376 publishes his thoughts on separating church and state. 1377 debate at St Paul's, London. Pope condemns his thinking. 1378 trial at Lambeth broken up by Londoners. 1381-2 condemned by church scholars. Forced into retirement, dies. 1428 body dug up and his remains destroyed.	**Charles V** **1364 - 1380**
Richard II **1377 – 1399**	**A sea change.** 1376, death of the Black Prince. 1377, English plunder Boulogne. Beginning of the Good Parliament, including the first election of a Speaker. Bad ministers sacked, for a time. French meanwhile sack Rye, Lewes, Folkestone, Plymouth, Isle of Wight. Death of Edward III. Hastings sacked. Charles V declares Brittany annexed but in so doing manages to unite both claimants against him. Brief English alliance with Navarre; English lease Cherbourg. 1380, vicious English raids on Brittany. Du Guesclin falls ill and dies. Charles V unexpectedly dies, leaving his son as a minor. **1378 Avignon Schism.** The French Cardinals leave Rome and return to Avignon under an anti-Pope **1380, The Peasants Revolt.** Third Poll tax. After previous problems, this one is levied on a per capita basis rather than a complicated grading on wealth: only paupers exempted. Three Essex villages refuse. King's men try to arrest the spokesman, Thomas Baker, but are beaten up. Chief Justice forced to swear he will desist, several jurors and clerks killed. Looting spreads across Essex and into west Kent. Rochester Castle captured. Rebels take Maidstone and appoint Wat Tyler their leader. Canterbury seized, some pillaging and murder. Emergence of John Ball the Mad Priest of Kent. Essex and Kent groups move on London. Royal prisons ransacked as is Lambeth Palace and John of Gaunt's home. First meeting between rebels and King. Tower of London seized, Archbishop of Canterbury and Treasurer	

	beheaded. Second royal meeting: Tyler punched to ground and knifed. King promises reforms on land and taxes to those present. Rebels disperse. Leaders caught and executed. Poll Tax abolished.	**Charles V** **1364 - 1380**
Richard II **1377 – 1399**	**Jockeyings for power.** 1382 Flemish urban independence movements largely crushed. English expedition to help Portugal vs Castile fails dismally. 1384 Duke of Burgundy inherits the lands of the Count of Flanders. 1385 (b) Aljubarrota: Portuguese smash Castilians, secure independence. John of Gaunt's invasion however fails, so a settlement is reached that at least takes the French ally out of the war. 1385-8 Franco-Scots raid English border, culminating in (b) Otterburn: Scots capture Henry 'Hotspur' Percy. 1386 Invasion scare. Massive French force awaits arrival of loitering late participants. Transiting troops devastate French countryside. Near-panic in parts of England, but delayed invasion finally cancelled at huge cost. Duke of Brittany switches sides after his captive competitor is set free.	**Charles VI** **1380 – 1422**
	Insanities in England. The Wonderful Parliament: the King is told if he seeks French aid against his own people he will be overthrown. 1387 **(b) Radcot Bridge**, Henry Bolingbroke defeats forces of Richard II who mostly drown. Lords Appellant – royal uncles opposed to Richard's advisers – dominant for a while but then outmanoeuvred. 1396 Long Truce agreed by Richard with France. Richard II marries a French princess, receives huge dowry, but French go cool on final territorial deal now the pressure is off, and are in any case preoccupied with a disastrous crusade in Hungary leading to their crushing defeat at **(b) Nicopolis** by the Turks. 1397, Richard II starts to brutally remove his opponents: uncle Duke of Gloucester is murdered. 1398, the Earl of March (the heir) is killed in a skirmish in Ireland. Richard II travels there to campaign. 1399 Bolingbroke, who had been exiled, invades. Richard II surrenders and abdicates. Bolingbroke crowned as Henry IV. Countercoup fails. 1400, Richard killed.	

Richard II **1377 – 1399**	**French madness.** 1392, Charles VI has his first 'turn' and attacks his own knights. 1393, a 'fancy dress' event at a ball goes horribly wrong as the costumes catch fire: the king narrowly survives. Periods of instability come and go. The King starts to believe he is made of glass and lets his appearance go. His Queen meanwhile appears to have an extended affair with the King's brother, leading to claims the future Dauphin is illegitimate.	**Charles VI** **1380 – 1422**
Henry IV **1399 - 1413**	**Borderland troubles.** 1400, Henry IV fails to force Scots into fealty. Owen Glendower (Owain Glyn Dwr) rises in North Wales. 1401 Glendower briefly captures Conway Castle. **(b) Pilleth:** Glendower badly defeats English near the border. 1402, Scots army defeated at **(b) Homildon Hill.** Royal decisions after the battles annoy the Percys who had been involved in both. Glendower conquers south Wales despite a huge English army. Sir Edmund Mortimer, captured at Pilleth but unransomed by the king, allies himself with Glendower. 1403 **(b) Shrewsbury:** those Percys who are in rebellion are crushed. French support arrives for Glendower, 1404 crowned Prince of Wales. French move on Aquitaine. Revolt fades, with Glendower's death a decade later.	
	Armagnacs vs Burgundians. Growing territorial power of Dukes of Burgundy. Disputes over who should be regent. 1407 Duke of Orleans assassinated. Duke of Burgundy flees Paris. A terrible winter. 1408 Burgundy pardoned by the King. 1411, Burgundy in control of Paris. Armagnacs besiege the capital. English send military assistance to Burgundians and break the siege. Both sides barter for English help. Armagnacs take control of Paris and the King.	

Low Season 1415 - 1453

This era is a season of huge glory for English adventurers, followed by a painful and slow decline ending in complete disaster. Don your armour, go out into the field, and pose for a brilliantly heroic oil painting.

King of England	Events	King of France
Henry V **1413 – 1422**	**Church Reconciled.** 1415, end of the papal schism.	**Charles VI** **1380 – 1422**
	Southampton Plot. 1415, attempt to kill Henry V	
	Lollards. 1413-1417 Sir John Oldcastle a Lollard in revolt. 1415 Council of Constance finally declares the movement a heresy. 1430s movement in decline, but survives locally until the Reformation. 1431 anti-clerical Perkyn's Uprising, quashed. is exposed.	
	Cry Havoc. 1415, Henry V and army lands near Harfleur. After a siege, the town is captured. French loyalists are expelled. Decision is taken to raid across to Calais ("chevauchée"). French army shadows, offering battle at **Agincourt**: massive English victory. 1417 surprise English descent on Caen, which is taken with bloodshed. 1418 uprising in Paris, much slaughter, Burgundians in control. 1419, Henry takes Rouen after terrible starvation of people trapped between the lines. Most of Normandy falls to English.	
	A Dauphin Dispossessed. Dauphin, the French heir, and his Armagnacs meet the Duke of Burgundy to reconcile. As the Duke kneels, he is murdered. His son openly supports the English. 1420 Henry V advances to Troyes. Treaty signed with the enfeebled French king: Dauphin dispossessed in favour of Henry, princess Catherine to marry Henry. French Queen declares her son the Dauphin illegitimate. Henry and Burgundy campaign together. They enter Paris.	

Henry V 1413 – 1422	**The death of kings.** 1421, Duke of Clarence – the King's brother - impetuously gives battle in the Loire Valley but is defeated and killed by a Franco-Scottish army. Henry campaigns south west of Paris, but falls ill and dies at Vincennes. Henry VI succeeds but is only a baby. Within a month, Charles VI too is dead. Henry's widow later secretly marries the ancestor of the Tudors.	Charles VI 1380 – 1422
	New Order. 1422 Regency Council formed in England. 1423, Dukes of Bedford, Brittany and Burgundy sign Treaty of Amiens vs Dauphin. Bedford, English Regent of France, marries Burgundy's sister. **(b) Cravant:** Anglo-Burgundian victory. 1424 Duke of Gloucester attempts to take certain territories in the Low Countries associated with his wife, but fails, and annoys Burgundy who is interested in this land. **(b) Verneuil,** another striking Anglo-Burgundian victory over Franco-Scots. Duke of Gloucester and Chancellor of England quarrel, threatening civil strife. 1427 Gloucester and his wife split, restoring Burgundian friendship. **(b) Montargis, (b) Ambrières** – French victories over English.	
Henry VI 1422 - 1461	**The crest of the wave.** 1428 advance on Orléans. On arrival, the English attackers are in fact outnumbered, but continue. They nearly force entry. A bombard is fired at the captured gatehouse in which the Earl of Salisbury is assessing the siege: he is badly mutilated and dies. 1429 **(b) of the Herrings:** Falstoff fights off an attack on a supply convoy.	Charles VII 1422 - 1461
	La Pucelle. 1429, Joan of Arc meets the Dauphin. She is green-lighted by Church review, and takes an army to Orléans. Siege fortifications are captured in turn. **(b) Patay,** Talbot captured in English defeat,	

Henry VI **1422 - 1461**	Orléans area secured. Dauphin advances on Rheims for formal coronation. 1430, Burgundians capture Joan at Compiègne. She is sold to the English and sent to Rouen. 1431 trial. Recants and given a life sentence. Retracts and executed.	**Charles VII** **1422 - 1461**

Ebbing English power. 1431 Henry VI crowned King of France, in Paris. Major English offensive falters. Franco-Burgundian 6 year truce. 1432 French successes in Chartres and Maine. 1433, Bedford and Burgundy drift apart after death of Bedford's Burgundian wife. 1434 English arm Norman peasants for self-protection against bandits: some revolt. 1435, **(b) Gerbevoy,** Earl of Arundel – a key English general – fatally wounded.

Grand peace conference at Arras. English reject the offer of Normandy and a royal marriage in exchange for surrendering claims on the French crown, and quit the talks. This proves utterly disastrous. In their absence, the Armagnacs and Burgundians make up. Charles apologises for killing the Duke's father; Burgundy given land and exempted from homage. Bedford dies. Burgundian-held territories are no longer under English control. Anti-Flemish riot in London. English sentiment pushes the war, despite their weak position, and its economy not being up to support the big garrisons required.

Reversal. 1435 loss of Dieppe, Harfleur and much of Normandy. 1436 loss of area around Paris, including Vincennes. **(b) Epinay:** Franco-Burgundians defeat small English field force. Paris captured by the French, who leave the Burgundians in the lead to soothe local concerns. French descent on Calais fails. 1437 Duke of York launches a counterattack which has some success, but fails due to angry peasants, Burgundian neutrality, French gunpowder and hostility at court. One bright spot for the English is that James I of Scotland fails to capture Roxburgh from the Earl of Northumberland and is soundly beaten. James is more successful in imposing his rule on his own lords, one of whom has him assassinated.

Henry VI 1422 - 1461		Charles VII 1422 - 1461

Battling decline. 1437 some English gains in Normandy, Rouen defended, Talbot victory at **(b) Ry. Burgundians** in turn pushed back by a swift Talbot strike. 1438 French advances in Aquitaine: Bordeaux almost falls. Terrible Starvation. 1437-1439 food scarcity in Europe, massive price rises, in some places laws passed that poor people must kill their dogs. Wolves in Paris streets. 1439 Oye peace conference: terrible English negotiating skills means a missed opportunity to retain territory, gain Normandy and possibly other land, a royal marriage, and ending homage in return for dropping the claim to the French throne. The war party in England stubbornly rejects peace. Pragueries: dissent as Charles suppresses private armies of his nobles. 1440, Duke of Orleans, last Agincourt prisoner, released but without concessions. English retake Harfleur. 1441 French take Pontoise by running away every time an English army appears, then returning to continue the siege afterwards. 1442, sudden French gains in the south. 1443, failed English campaign in Normandy. 1444, Treaty of Tours. Henry to marry Charles's niece, Margaret of Anjou, with a truce. But no dowry and not to a senior royal, and with a hidden price of surrendering claims to Maine. Court intrigues in England increase: fall of Henry's uncle the Duke of Gloucester (1447). 1448, English troops reticent to quit Le Mans in Maine as per the treaty terms, until French army appears. 1449, The former garrison goes rogue and ends up sacking Fougères. French end the ceasefire and launch a massive invasion of Normandy. English badly prepared and led: Rouen and most of duchy lost. 1450 English relief army attacks one French army but is then hit on a flank by an arriving Breton one at **(b) Formigny.** Normandy is lost, Cherbourg holding out the last. Recriminations begin in England.

Jack Cade's Rebellion. 1450, a disciplined insurrection leads to a force swiftly outside of London. Their demands are fair for the times, but a royal army is levied. It is defeated. London wavers and Cade arrives. Some former royal advisers executed. Discipline breaks down and Londoners

Henry VI 1422 - 1461	...start to fight. Royal pardons arrive and Cade's forces shrink. Cade defeated and killed. 1451 more stirrings in Kent and Wiltshire suppressed. Henry VI looks weak, Yorkist alternative looking better..	Charles VII 1422 - 1461
	The End. 1451, French attack Aquitaine across the whole front. Collapse. Bordeaux surrenders: citizens allowed to leave for England, or stay and accept French rule. 1452, Richard Duke of York makes an armed bid for power: he fails but is spared. Birth of a royal heir, Prince Edward, removes York from the immediate line of succession, making him expendable. 1452, Duke of Burgundy considers financing English against a resurgent France. Bordeaux rises in revolt and Talbot arrives with English force. 1453 on being reinforced, he marches to relieve the besieged Castillon. Victory in an initial skirmish. The English then blunder into a larger force, dug in, with cannons; a large force of Breton reinforcements arrives and hits them in the flank. Talbot killed. English forces are now clearly on the defensive, heavily outnumbered, and for the first time facing formidable artillery that changes the rules and timetables of siege warfare. Bordeaux surrenders. Henry VI falls into madness. The Wars of the Roses are at hand.	

Out of Season

King of England	Events
Henry VIII	Tudor expeditions result in short-term possession of Tournai and Boulogne, but these expensive victories do not endure. Some plotting to invade Bordeaux and stir revolt, but impractical and never actioned.
Mary I	1558. Final loss of Calais to the French ends ancient English holdings on the continent.
George III	1763. Britain wins Québec from the French, which has many settlers from regions once held by the English Crown. Their old accents later survive thanks to being cut off from France while regional identities are suppressed by

	Paris. Bordeaux merchants complain to the French King about the loss of their trade access to Canada and fail in their lobby to get the province back in the peace talks.
	1801. **The Treaty of Amiens** (briefly) brings peace between the United Kingdom and post-Revolutionary France. One of the stipulations is that the Hanoverians renounce their claim to the French throne. The exiled Jacobite pretenders incidentally do not sign up to this, so technically they still have a claim if ever there is a restoration of the Stuart dynasty.
Elizabeth II	1953. An International Court confirms that the Minquiers and Ecréhous, uninhabited island groups off Jersey, belong to the UK Crown. Hundred Years Wars treaties are cited. Despite further agreement in 2000 setting out territorial waters, disputes remain over fisheries.

Travelling Safely

Walking is so pedestrian.

Driving

Wagons, carts and carriages are available for wheeled transport. You will probably be better off walking or on horseback, as roads are poor and the (lack of decent) suspension will be killing you.

Drive on the left. Or maybe the right. But just get out of the way of important people wearing armour who are in a hurry.

Bastides

Especially found in the French south, **bastides** are new towns that have been set up, often in commanding parts of the countryside. They may be local commercial centres and market places for the rural economy. Expect a fairly central square, well-planned streets, regulated housing, and if the locals are sensible some sturdy walls. They may have lower taxes imposed on them in order to encourage settlement, and they elect their own magistrates, sometimes pretentiously reusing various Roman titles.

These villages can often be useful places to break a journey and many are attractive places to visit in their own right.

Health and insurance

The world is a dangerous place. If you are a trader we recommend joining a guild to maintain the well-being of your dependents in the case of your unfortunate demise.

Merchants coming by sea from Italy may be disappointed by the lack of developed maritime insurance to cover for lost shipping: it is recommended you make these arrangements before you travel. If passing by Brittany, a prior indemnity can be bought from the Duke (or if inconvenienced, his English garrison commander) so that if your ship runs aground on its rocky coast, he has already agreed to forfeit his right to salvage. This means you don't lose the lot.

Leprosy has become a problem since the crusades. Many will be looked after by the Church, but some do wander the streets seeking alms. If you see people dressed in distinctive clothing, waving a bell or clappers, run like the latter.

Wilderness survival
Tip one: look blindingly obviously like a non-combatant. Tip two: bring food

Social class

Class matters. Class provides privilege. It's an indicator of wealth. It's a route to power.

Take a hobby as straightforward as birdwatching, or as it's known locally, falconry. There is a strict hierarchy of who can own what kind of bird of prey to go hunting for sport or for your supper. The best birds, after all, are rare, extraordinarily expensive, high maintenance, and require considerable effort to train. Emperors can use eagles; kings the white gyr falcon; greater nobles the peregrine falcon; knights are permitted sakers if they could get hold of one; ladies can use merlins (falconry is after all a multi-sex sport); priests are permitted the sparrowhawk; yeomen can use goshawks; while those clinging desperately to the bottom rung on life's ladder can keep a kestrel – which is fine if you like to nibble on half-chewed dormice.

Happily, these lands are more or less free from slavery. It did exist at the time of the Norman Conquest of England, but social changes have meant a new form of relationship emerging between masters and the oppressed.

The ordinary class of working folk in England are the peasants. But their lot differs. Those who are their own masters, because they have a trade or own their own land, are freemen. They have special protection thanks to the Magna Carta. Those who are dependent are serfs. They are attached to a tract of land, and work it in return for protection from their lord, for

instance in times of crop failure or banditry. They may be expected to pay a local tax to him called a chevage. If the land is sold, they are also passed on as a going concern. Of course, this quite literally rather limits their horizons. It's a condition few aspire to, but bondage beats starving to death. The condition is inherited. Villeins on the other hand are peasants with a better deal. They pay rent, and may owe some duties to their landowner such as helping out during harvest time, but otherwise can get on with their lives in their own time.

With the poorer becoming gradually wealthier, the terms of these arrangements are getting rewritten over time. The trend jumps massively thanks to the plague epidemics and the terrible impact on the population. More land is free, more replacement workers are needed to sow and bring in the harvests, and so it becomes a labourers' market. With strong competition between landowners to employ people, the result is better standards and higher wages. It will take some time but a huge shift in society is taking place, and the poorer in society are seeing an increase in wealth, standing, freedom, and importance. The impact will stretch across the board; you can see hints of it in the development of the democratic system, in the emergence of a broader middle class and a countryside gentry, and perhaps too in the growth of individualism and free thought. Survive the sword and the buboes and it's a fascinating time to be around.

Nevertheless, even if it's evolving radically at the bottom, social class does still count. Notwithstanding the niceties of law, the word of the king still runs writ and he can lop your head off and worry about a legal challenge after the event.

Remember that there are respectful and also familiar ways of talking to someone in English and in French – misspeak a 'tu' instead of 'vous', or 'thee' instead of 'ye', and you are in for a bruising. Monarchs should be called 'Highness'/'Altesse', though 'Excellence' is an alternative at the French court - which may or may not be accurate but that's an observation not worth risking either.

Witchcraft

First, it's important to make a distinction between sorcery and household cures. For instance, it is common knowledge that to cure someone bitten by a dog, you have to take a crust of bread and write on it "Bestera bestie nay brigonay dictera sagragan es domina fiat fiat fiat". This is not witchcraft, it's just old tradition.

Still, the Church does get jittery at times so it may be best not to make too much of it. Many local problems and crises can be ascribed to having a witch in the vicinity. As everyone knows, these are evil women who in return for selling themselves to the Infernal One, have been granted impossible powers. Don't be duped by soft words and false claims that they just know a little about various herbs and shrubs and some first aid. These are invariably minions of Beelzebub and his legions of infernal imps, and merit no pity.

Signs of having a witch in the area include;
- Crop failure
- Ill people
- Flying women spotted at night, probably laughing evilly
- Missing children
- Sightings of wild nocturnal parties in secluded locations involving nakedness and amphibians
- Talking goats

Signs of someone being a witch include;
- A woman being old
- Spots
- Suspicious headgear
- Excessive affinity to household cleaning equipment
- The individual talking to themselves
- Saying bad things about someone who then falls ill
- Ownership of a cat, or other familiar, used to communicate with the Devil
- Being very ugly, since evil shows its true face
- Not being very ugly, since evil can hide its true form
- Having a part of the body where she can feel no pain when prodded
- Not being easily killed when put to the test, eg by drowning
- Admitting to witchcraft under threat or actual use of torture

While these sorceresses can predict the future, avoid associating with them as we can also predict theirs.

The Black Death

There are two things you need as a traveller to know about the Bubonic Plague. Firstly, it is very black. Secondly, it is very deadly.

There is little hope outrunning it, as it seems to travel as fast as a man on a speeding horse.

Your best chance from what little we know about this dreadful plague from God is to live an upright life, pray a lot, and avoid touching anything those affected have touched. Wash coins, for example.

The crisis arrives from Italy, thanks to Genoese ships trading with afflicted Crimea. It is carried across to southern France and over the following year spreads north.

At least it's quick.

Symptoms include;

- Big black swellings under the arms and on the groin, which might leak
- Internal bleeding
- Sweating
- Coughing
- An evil odour
- Utter despair

Death follows four or five days after initial diagnosis, but can be as swift as the same day in bad cases where a fever takes hold.

When it strikes, thousands upon thousands will die. It will keep coming back and back. The second wave is even worse, spreads even more readily, and is an even greater killer. You cannot hide; it migrates across the land.

Our book can offer you no hope other than to trust in divine protection and luck, to observe the prospect of symptoms in the community around you, and perhaps to make sure you get cash on delivery.

Working Out an Itinerary

Public holidays

Expect little opportunity for serious tourism on public holidays, most notably where there is a celebration ongoing, such as during a royal wedding. More frequently, travellers may find themselves out and about on feast days. There are lots.

Each celebrates a saint or a religious event, and indeed help act as a measurement of time or calendar. Key days fall at Easter, May, June and December. A celebratory feast would be followed by a holiday, with an exceptionally long one in December (though as it's not growing season and can be cold outside, that may be no loss). Perhaps one day in twelve might be worthy of a day off, particularly as far as a relevant patron saint is concerned or for the anniversary of some important biblical event.

Sundays

In addition to the feast days, expect Sundays to be a day of rest.

Fasting

These details may be useful for gastronauts.

On certain days you may find it impossible to get served meat. It's meant to be a fast. Eating red meat is forbidden: however, fish doesn't count so you can tuck into seafood instead.

These Fish Days are mainly just Fridays but you might find some observing them on Wednesdays also.

The period of Lent is also traditionally used for fasting.

Opening hours

Anticipate shops being open during daylight, later if trade is good and guilds allow. Rural life may begin earlier depending on the needs of the farm.

Mechanical clocks are rare and typically confined to cathedrals. Salisbury, Wells, Rouen and Paris provide some effective late fourteenth century timepieces. Accurate waterclocks and time candles are not much more common. Sundials are less than practical for the tourist on the go. However, church services take place at set times of the day so keep an ear open for church bells if time is important for you.

The day isn't generally measured by the 24 hour clock until the clocks began to appear, in the last quarter of the fourteenth century. Before then, mark time using the canonical hours of the church;

- Matins, variably set at some time between midnight and dawn
- Prime, sunrise
- Terce, third hour of the morning
- Sixt, mid day
- Nones, mid afternoon
- Vespers, late afternoon
- Compline, evening

These are of course largely focused on daylight hours, which vary according to the season and latitude.

Getting around

There is no public transport as such. Buy a horse.

Accommodation

Servcie can be poor on a busy day.

Inns are widespread, provide accommodation, and serve food. By contrast, taverns are drinking places but might serve snacks. Note that outside of the towns and away from the guilds, some taverns are simply private houses selling home brew, so mind the cat when you sit down.

Both exist in sufficient numbers and spread to provide a fairly safe guarantee of home comforts during your trip, though when travelling between towns it might be worth double checking where the next way point will be and reaching it before nightfall. Prices should be affordable, though factor in a roof for your horse round the back as well.

Those in larger towns on business might exceptionally seek to be accommodated by the relevant guild or, if your links are good, amongst your expat community. People travelling on official business might seek hospitality from local grandees instead. Budget travellers should remember that the Church, and in particular its monasteries, has a long tradition of putting up travellers, particularly those on pilgrimages.

Vagrancy is a crime, so don't try sleeping in ditches, and then looking as if you just have.

Since the famine years of the 1310s and the 1330s, and the rural depression that followed, you'll find that France is a real bargain for travellers. Lodgings are cheap. So too is food, but do allow for interruptions to the local food supply if there is military activity in the neighbourhood. Sieges can make the cost of living frighteningly expensive.

Toilets

In housing in built up areas, one relieves oneself into a receptacle. This is emptied out of the window at a time of convenience. As housing on upper storeys overhangs the street, it is customary to give a warning to passers by below: in England this is now something approaching "Gardez loo", a derivation from the original French instruction to look out for the incoming water.

If you hear it, step swiftly to one side and pray you avoid splash.

Food and Drink

Food

The Roman Empire caused the spread of much of what constitutes a spread, some of which was actually spread. But what led to the spread is now dead.

While a number of the plants and animals the Romans originally brought with them came to flourish in their new environment, it has taken quite some time for other foodstuffs to reappear on the plate only now thanks to improving trade links with far off climes. Other produce which may be familiar to exotic travellers won't be spotted round these parts at all.

Let's start with what you won't find. Sweet jungle nuts, underground starch tubules, and squishy red fruits are too far away for anyone even to dream about. Large hairy hard shell nuts might get washed up after a storm but are curios best used in artwork. Bananas are exotic southern foods and very unlikely to be spotted round these parts, and the same goes for peaches unless you have the money. Forget eastern habits with coffee and tea. Spices will cost you a fortune, as will peppers, but salt is all around. It might not be white though if the householder hasn't had time to boil it.

Happily, that still leaves lots of excellent local produce. Cheese, for example, abounds, and there are no fewer than several different varieties. Chestnuts, almonds and walnuts contribute to healthy living. Vegetables are widely consumed, though are less sought after than meat if you can afford it. If in humbler company, prepare your palette for a plain vegetable or even fruit starter, and a main course that might feature turnips, beans, cress, onions, leeks, mushrooms and carrots. There are also peas, which for some peculiar and utterly unknown reason people find hilariously funny just to mention by name. Shelling them therefore risks starting a comedy routine. Amongst fruit, aim for cherries and other woodland fare.

If your vegetable is talking to you, cover up your ears immediately. It is a mandrake and its scream might kill you.

Bread is an increasingly important accompaniment. Butter is available, but often preferred on fish days. Eggs can be popular. Rice is a safe option.

Frumenty is a sort of wheat broth. Pastry is sometimes used to provide a different approach: pies tend to be large, meaty and spacious. They often feature quite lean cuts since the fat often goes into other dishes that require stock. For some reason, veal pasties need extra beef fat put in them so they are not one for weight watchers.

Meats include rabbit, mutton, ham, beef, goat, boar, and venison. These include backbone, tongue and offal dishes. Salted mustard tongue is a favourite in Gascony. The more adventurous, or desperate, can try squirrel or hedgehog pie.

Fish include pike, carp, plaice, sole, herring, cod, mackerel and (cautiously) the sting ray. The best eel is especially shiny and has a small head: we recommend you stew it. Scallops are tasty. Eat only fresh oysters and when in season. Lobsters are also recommended.

Geese are amongst the types of bird you might eat. Those raised in Paris are fed on a gruel made of flour and oats so if you can spot a difference in taste locally, that might explain it. You can also have chicken, duck, pigeon or even larks. Herons are a peculiar exotic alternative, but we counsel not serving them; they are a symbol of temerity and the diner might think you are making a statement.

If you can name it, you can probably afford it.

Pomegranites will be more expensive, as will bitter Spanish oranges which can also be found on sale in Paris.

Sauces should be strained and soups left with all its components. Gosling soup, for instance, should still have the little birds in it to be served.

Pots or complex plates could be garnished with various local herbs. Mustard, for instance, can be added to cooking oil and bread cubes.

Amongst the better dishes are veal pies, black puddings, sausages, partridges, waterfowl, bacon gruel, Lombard tarts (which have small birds in them), lampreys, crayfish, beef kebabs, or even boar's head. Meat or fish may be provided as a sort of jelly. We have even heard of dishes made up of heron, peacock, bittern, and astonishingly "caponised falcon". This sounds either like a true extravagance, or the perfect cover for a servant's accident with the bird cage. Barely less surprising you can even find people recommending porpoise, though this is obviously a fish so is a rich choice for a Friday. For dessert, plump for the cream flan.

Note that much of the produce will be extremely local. Out in the countryside, your host may well have not only with his or her own hands made the boar sausage, but killed the boar. If dining in high society, avoid what look like squidgy fingers served with bread. Even if they are well washed and flavoured, they are still snails.

Drink

The staple drink is very weak ale - indeed it can be part of a man's set wages, and is safer than the water. Happily for the social drinker, there is stronger stuff out there too. In the fifteenth century, hopped beers start to be introduced to England in quantity from the continent, and then hops themselves as part of the malting process. By the end of the Low Season the initial reticence against this bitter new taste is being overcome and this strong ale, or beer, starts to get a real foothold. But bear in mind too that in periods of famine and poor harvests, such as 1437-1439, just as bread becomes ten times more expensive so too will you find your favourite beverage hit – in some places bans on beer are brought in.

If beer's not your thing, go for the cider instead. Locally, you might find some places serving mead. Far more common however is wine: this is not just from the English territories overseas, as thanks to the Portuguese alliance special rates are provided to encourage the import of Portugal's best, especially port. Run out of red wine to serve your guests? Fear not: a well-versed host will know the trick to colour white wine to match the dish.

Strong drinks are not for everyone. If illness limits you to a few mouthfuls of porridge, accompany it with some milk. There's also for sick people the sweet barley water known as the tisane, or you can go for the boiled hazelnut or almond cordial, or again simply sit down with a mug of stock.

What about the drinking water? Urban areas will have access to steady supplies. These will sometimes be wells but while the age of the aqueducts may have passed into memory, the Roman alternative of piping water in from sources out of town does still sometimes survive, thanks to the health-bringing properties of lead piping. Sometimes special tunnels and passageways are dug to accommodate the piping, and allow access to them to fix leaks.

Dining

Dining is a social occasion. The best of them can take place over many courses and if a celebration perhaps even over successive days. If a basin is offered, wash your hands in it before starting. In posh company, an earthenware or metal pouring pot called an aquamanile acts as a ewer.

Let's hope you don't end up at the scale of event where each guest has a tun of wine set aside for their own personal use. Expect three or four services for a real lunch, though a couple of these may be supplied as a side dish. Dinner might be just the three plates. Don't hold out for anything too extravagant in an inn unless your purse can reach that far. A dessert and then some spiced wine should round the evening off when amongst the best company, all accompanied by some good music and conversation.

Food is eaten from a piece of stale bread (then eaten or given away) or from a plate, often wooden, called a trencher. This should be supplied by your host, but bring your own knife, and wooden spoon just to be safe. Drinks are supplied in bowls.

Style and Fashion

What to wear

With rank comes power. So it's important not to dress inappropriately, which might be seen as imposture. Equally, under-dressing is something that can give people the wrong impression about you, something to avoid unless you happen to be on the run and do need to look like a dishevelled monk.

This period sees a transformation in styles away from old fashioned cloaks and robes and bodices and into more localised looks. But the overall division of garments remains the same. A man of any substance wears footwear, stockings or lower leg wear, breeches with belt, a coat or shirt, an overcoat, and something on his head. Cloaks and capes are also available and provide protection against the elements.

The well-dressed man about town is typically the one sacking it.

The French especially take great pride in their clothing, to the point of picking the best quality materials and throwing jewels on to them, and wearing clothes far too small or too tight for them. The Duke of Burgundy in particular is a real fashion leader at court; and this at a court that's so expensive that its embassies need special taxes raised just to cover the ambassador's outfits and expenses. After a while English embassies sensibly give up trying to compete, save the taxpayer the money, and just turn up looking casual in travel gear or armour.

However, ermine and sable do remain closely associated with the nobility. There are attempts by the merchant classes to rise above their station and sumptuary laws are passed to hinder this. Ordinary people will just have to wear whatever their wagon accidentally runs over.

Thus, examples of prohibitions on clothing in England include in 1363;

- Grooms, servants, and apprentices to have clothing made from cloth worth no more than 2 Marks
- Silk, silver and gold embroidery, and veils worth more than twelve pence, forbidden to them and their families
- Yeomen and artisans to have a limit of cloth worth 40 shillings; no gold or silver bling or gemstones
- No silk veils for their family; only furs made out of lamb, rabbit, fox or cat
- Gentlemen and rich merchants to have a limit of 4½ Marks to have no purple, to be allowed some silver furnishings, and basic fur and head jewellery for the women
- Knights to be allowed 6 Marks and forbidden gold but allowed head jewellery, or pearls for the women
- Clerics with a university degree would be allowed the privileges of a knight of the same estate
- Carters, ploughmen and herders to be limited to twelvepence worth of linen – no cloth except for a blanket, and to eat in an appropriate and not excessive manner
- Gold and silk are reserved for the royals
- Foreigners to be prohibited from importing silk and lace (to better restrict sales to the right sort of people: but unfortunate for you if you a trader)
- Clothing is liable to be confiscated if found to be worn above the wearer's station

By the fifteenth century, shoulder pads start to come into fashion. Wear them if you must. Try to avoid the commoners' trend to emphasise groin coverings in the trouser wear.

With rank comes not just the right to ostentation, but the expectation of it too. You might find people accused of having enough wealth and land to dress and live like a knight, but choosing not to. This is highly frowned on by the Court, but quite widespread. Laws are sometimes passed threatening large fines if they don't assume their rightful standing, a process known as distraint of knighthood.

Women's Clothing

Cross dressing is considered blasphemous, and as bad as impersonating someone of a different social rank. So pick your costume with care if you want to avoid Joan of Arc's fate.

Nets are often worn as part of a headdress, while leggings are not worn but a form of skirt is.

Such clothing is less prone to the excesses of the male peacock over the years: while it becomes more richly adorned, it is also shortened to become more practical. On the other hand, high cones start to come into fashion. Avoid the temptation to use them in hoop games.

Underwear

So long as the little fellow stays under control in a banquet, no one will ask. You will be wearing at least one layer over the crucial bits anyway with your breeches.

Footwear

Shoes tend to be pointy these days, and as this shocks priests, tend to get even more pointy when disputes with the Church break out. If your interlocutor walks like a seal, he may well be a heretic. The better class of person might well snigger at the pointiest of these Crakows, so named as the fashion has lately been reimported from Polish parts.

Footwear, which is typically leather but exceptionally might be textile, comes in a variety of forms, just as the shape of your foot requires.

You can also look at the wooden kind. Pattens are basic overshoes designed as mini-stilts to allow people to walk above the level of grime on the streets. It's not inconceivable you might spot someone in clogs, shoes made entirely out of wood that offer some increased protection.

Hair

The fourteenth century sees olds trends of long hair and heroic beards somewhat tamed. The Old Testament style loses its charm. You might find hair in France by the fifteenth century still growing amply but only down to the neck, and beards and moustaches frowned on. By contrast, a practical field soldier like Henry V aims for a soup bowl look, which while less stylish is a much better match for a helmet. But beards and 'taches are still out for those who aren't old-style warlords.

Well-off women conceal their hair in wimples and side nets. These become very complex with time, by the fifteenth century becoming incorporated into the design of various hats where it's difficult to spot where the hair ends and the curtain begins. The steeple hats come in very late in the Low Season: don't try importing them before then.

Information Technology

Communications

Basic messages can be sent by beacons, set up along the coast during times of invasion scare. These are somewhat simpler than during Roman times, mainly limited to a message about the enemy having arrived. Watchtowers can be innovatively improvised by stacking wine barrels filled with sand.

Larger settlements tend to have town criers, whose principle function is to make public announcements of local or national importance. It's possible they'll be announced by a trumpeter. The texts would then end up posted somewhere for people to subsequently read, typically nailed to the church door or in the village square. In busy settlements listen out at major intersections.

Do not heckle or jostle as you may end up arrested for impeding an officer of the Crown in the line of his work. For that matter, avoid distributing official material from the other side in the wrong place.

For the latest unofficial word, you might try one of the guilds in case a member has recently returned from travel, or buying someone from out of town a pint at an alehouse. Ports and harbours are excellent for international gossip, as even in war time fishermen from both sides openly discuss the latest developments in the neutral setting of their shared work space out at sea. If preparations for an expedition are under way though, be mindful that departures may be prohibited from ports until invasion fleets have departed: factor in delays to your travel arrangements.

The Media

The moveable type, or modifiable, printing press is invented by Gutenburg right at the very end of the Low Season. At this time Caxton over in England is still trading in wool. There is no Media.

The rise of the university

Despite the limits of this communications world, an important development has taken place since the Dark Ages with the establishment of the university.

Oxford and Cambridge have been going in their current form since the thirteenth century. A spur was the war with France, which kept students from learning there. France's places of learning are Paris, Montpellier, Toulouse, and now Poitiers (1431).

In Scotland, St Andrews (1413) and later Glasgow (1451) are also founded.

Such places of learning have expanded to provide for a variety of fields of study. These are essentially theology, canon law, civil law, medicine, and the arts, though locally reputations in different fields vary across time. The influence of the Church in their founding remains strong, and indeed lecturers and students are considered to be part of the system of Holy Orders that puts them under the jurisdiction of the Church rather than of the local townspeople.

There can be a very strong 'them and us' feeling that grows out of this. In Cambridge for example, the town once had such a reputation for overcharging students for accommodation that the King intervened. Since then, the university has come to actually own large chunks of the town. Anti-student riots kick off three times in the fourteenth century. Happily though things aren't as bad as what happened back in 1272, when a fight between students from the North and from the South escalated badly and the locals piled in. The net result of that back then was a number of locals were hanged. If you are coming to these parts as a student, be aware that these tensions are still there and can lead to bloodshed - so even if you are protected by privilege and law, it might not protect you from a lump of wood.

Internal squabbles can also generate friction. A new university was set up in Northampton for northern students, a move that split both Oxford and Cambridge and was linked to the riot mentioned above. As it happened, Northampton University wouldn't last because the students shortly afterwards took the wrong side in a siege involving the King, but once again half of Oxford University upped sticks in 1333 and spent a couple of years in exile in Stamford.

So be aware of student politics, as it can have some very serious implications.

Law and Disorder

Crime

There is a great difference between engaging in a plundering expedition under a royal banner, and tagging along for a ride with a thug. The first is permitted, subject to the rules and niceties of war – indeed your actions are covered by law. The second however is just downright thievery. You need some form of official status to your crimes.

Robbery and kidnapping become increasingly a problem for travellers over this period, particularly when things are going badly for a monarch.

His prestige wanes; his troops are less effective at maintaining the peace; the Crown demands more taxes and can spend it on less; trade routes are fractured; the currency itself becomes debased, and prices go up; people become impoverished and driven to break the law; morals and human restraints are broken. You'll see it over much of France, and at the close in remoter parts of England. The most extreme example is where rebellions break out, particularly those that rampage against those better off in society.

In those environments, hide your chattels, look poor, and try not to draw attention to yourself as an outsider and therefore someone to blame.

We would counsel travelling more by ship, except that piracy is almost a second profession in a surprising number of ports and even a primary money raiser for some lords who live by the sea. As a neutral outsider, at least in England there is a chance that the Crown may recompense you for your losses. The chance is far stronger though that if it comes to trial, the pirate himself will get off scot free in the Admiralty Court due to a supposed lack of evidence.

You have more chance though fighting back against petty crime. If you are a victim and the criminal goes on the run, head to a sheriff and ask him to form a posse comitatus. A Hue and Cry is a more ad hoc arrangement where you (or a witness) call on the spot for assistance from local residents to apprehend the miscreant, for whom they share some legal responsibility as fellow locals. With luck, you can put together a helpful mob to capture the felon. A false Hue and Cry is, it is to be noted, a criminal offence.

Note also that if an illegal act is going on, the victim can shout out and call for legal intervention: this is called the Clameur de Haro. We suggest a simple raising of the voice and asking for an official will do the trick in a market dispute, but don't abuse it to try to knock a farthing off a price.

Legal matters

Outside of the merchant guilds, local government falls into the hands of dedicated officers. There's no set model. England has sheriffs while in France there's a more direct line in managing the law. Sheriffs are appointed by the Crown, or often in practice local bigwigs, to maintain law and order. In some cases you might find the post being elected locally. This can be a sticking point. A sheriff is only as good as he is independent, and someone who is in the thrall or even pay of a noble in the neighbourhood is unlikely to give you much of a sympathetic hearing if you complain about him or against his interests. It may be worth taking a clearly bad case of abuse to Westminster though, as sheriffs are meant to be impartial and they are subject to disciplinary control.

In addition to the Sheriff's court, there will be a local court dealing with property rights and minor criminal cases. You may find some judicial posts and responsibilities go automatically with people owning or renting certain tracks of land.

Out in the countryside, ancient court leets or halimotes have long existed for village gentry to try minor offences amongst their tied serfs. These meet regularly and cover those peasants who are dependent upon the master of the manor. Free peasants can access the royal courts.

There's another old system called the frankpledge, allowing for sureties for good behaviour by landed folk, or joint bonds by the landless – meaning that people are jointly responsible if one of their number has committed a wrong. That system is fading away as constables take a greater role along with Justices, bringing in law from the outside.

The post of mayor becomes increasingly important, though the role may often look ill-defined. A town that gets a royal charter, however, is definitely on the up. That means many of the cases formerly heard in the royal court get transferred to local jurisdiction.

Essentially what we are seeing over this period is power shifting towards courts and agents set up and sent out by the Crown. There's a standardisation of the law, and perhaps more of a sense of impartial fairness slowly creeping in. You might also sense that lawyers are becoming more important, which means having to find the money for fees, at least for the bigger cases.

Note that if arrested during your visit, torture will likely only be used to extract a confession if there are some pointers that you are guilty, or more likely once a guilty verdict has been secured by the court. There is an ingenious array of tools at your interrogators' disposal. Most will only surface if treason is involved: unlike for instance Scotland, England is emerging as a judicial system that steps away from commonly using torture to determine guilt. By contrast, methods of punishment are less innovative. Imprisonment is only used for holding people awaiting trial or ransom; fines, physical punishment and executions are possible penalties. Stocks submit criminals to public humiliation. But let's not dwell on the unpleasant side: you can visit a torture chamber if the subject fascinates you and look at an unchristian mass of instruments of pain that create an orchestra of woe.

The law is biased in favour of the better sort of person, who are, after all, most likely to uphold it, and most in the eye of the king if they do not. So if considering bringing charges against a baron for not paying a bill of two shillings, remember that members of the English nobility can appeal to have their case held in the House of Lords, judged by their peers. They also have a right of access to the King to raise issues of concern with him. Furthermore, under the principles of scandalum magnatum, they have a degree of protection approaching that of the king against libel, meaning that even if an allegation is true you had better be able both to prove it and show it's in the general interest to say it, as otherwise you are undermining public confidence in great men. It's a crazy and dangerous law, but don't get caught saying it.

Remember above all else that you are a visitor and not a diplomat. Merchants are not immune from the law, and indeed sometimes are not protected by it. In the 1340s for example, the English arrest French merchants, and the French in response arrest all English residents. The French also seize all Italian moneylenders, and their property, including the titles on their loans. Be careful where you are during this heated period.

Church courts

If on the run for a crime that you didn't commit, if nobody else can help, and if you can find one, then maybe you can hide with the nave team. Thanks to the privilege know as the Benefit of Clergy, churches are covered by a separate legal system, and can offer sanctuary to those on the run. In some places you need to sit down on a special stone seat to claim it, in others to grab hold of the door knocker, and if there's any doubt your best bet may be to grab hold of the altar and make your application absolutely clear. There's still no guarantee that an angry chasing mob or fired-up band of soldiery will apply the niceties.

As we've already seen with the universities, those in holy orders are also protected by the Church, which can include a very loose affiliation with the institution indeed. The clergy run their own court system, quite separate from all the other courts operating out there. Peculiars are local church courts that occupy a similar position to the courts of the Lord of the Manor. Archdeaconry courts are the usual first court. The consistories are the bishops' courts, sometimes divided into commissary courts. The Archbishops have several higher forms of court of their own. There is a right of appeal to Rome, or these days Avignon – the supreme court is called the Rota.

There is a definite advantage to being tried by this system. Punishments are designed to reinstall moral fibre and rescue the soul, since the Church frowns on its members drawing blood. You might also be barred from attending services, which risks your place in the afterlife. Such corporeal leniency doesn't apply if you are an unrepentant heretic .

Civil magistrates might test the arraigned criminal before he's handed over to see if he is trying to pull a fast one: a favoured technique is to pick a biblical verse and see if the suspect can quote it. Alternatively, for judges who don't want to apply a harsh sentence, it can also be a way of getting someone off your hands without having to apply a death penalty. But otherwise, these courts manage issues such as wills, rowdiness on Church property or on the Sabbath, missing Church services, sexual immorality, illegitimacy, and marriage – hopefully not all in the same case.

Trial by ordeal

Law is not reserved just for man's judgement, as a party can put himself in God's hands to demonstrate the merits of his case.

Here there are different types, dependent on the quality of the accused. Trial by combat is as a rule overwhelmingly reserved for knights, with victory being reserved for the just side. Water can be used either to test innocence by allowing the accused to float without swimming, most fairly achieved if not bound and weighed down; it can also be heated up for the accused to immerse an arm in to see if he or she gets scalded. Trial by fire means the party walking over or holding heated iron. Rare these days is the huge get-out clause for the clergy and our favourite: Trial by bread, and seeing if you choke when having a holy wafer.

Don't count on being allowed to appeal to it these days. A few too many oxes of knights have gotten away with obvious murder over the years.

Religion

The Church

The territories of France and Britain overwhelmingly adhere to the Catholic faith. This institution is represented locally in the parish church, and these are certainly worth visiting because of the significant range in their design. The spindly spires that rise upwards out of England's Fens are very different from the solid slightly squat hulks of Picardy, and the very hue of the stones in the north of England sometimes add an imposing grimness that contrasts with the pale forms of Rouen.

However, there's more to the Church than just the buildings, and it's important to remember that when filing into a cathedral for a quick look around.

The Great Schism

Just as it's impolite to discuss politics with your host, especially in the midst of a massive war, you may well find religion a particularly divisive subject. This is because the Church is undergoing a huge crisis right now.

In 1305, a Bordeaux Archbishop was elected Pope as Clement V. His priorities lay north of the Alps and he never made it to Rome. That wasn't so strange, as while that city was the notional headquarters of the Church, for many years Popes have often stayed away from it. It's a tiny town these days filled with ruins and squabbles. But Clement chose to settle at Avignon in 1309, and thanks to the rough state of Italy, his successors followed his example. Sitting on the very frontier of French royal territory, and indeed later with a royal fortress within sight of their palace, this proves very handy for the French monarch in trying to influence affairs within the Church.

Urban V briefly returns to Rome in 1365, but he comes back to Avignon. His successor Gregory XI pledges to go back but dies shortly after arriving, and probably not far from leaving it again. For his replacement, and menaced by the Rome mob, the cardinals are swiftly pressured into picking an Italian Archbishop, Urban VI. He proves to be a somewhat testy character. The French cardinals (of whom there are by now many) quit the city, elect one of their own as Clement VII in 1378, and return to Avignon. Thus you now have a Pope, and an anti-Pope. Which one is which I leave to the tavern discussions to settle. But the Avignon story moves into a new phase.

France and its allies support the Avignon pope. The opponents of the French King support the papacy in Rome. Thus in Britain, your head of church will change depending on whether you are inside or outside the gates of Berwick. Add a mix of other countries that are neutral in the conflict but have views of their own and you have a confusing mix. Leading church figures that will in time become saints themselves take both sides. The successors of these two popes prove even more obstinate.

In 1409 at Pisa, Church leaders meet to settle the matter. They resolve to annul the existing popes and recognise a third. Unfortunately, neither existing pope agrees to stand down, and so there are now three popes. Only at the Council of Constance in 1414 are two popes sacked and the third resigns, and in 1417 a replacement to all three, Martin V, elected.

That would be that, but another antipope will pop again at the close of the Low Season. Martin V had set up the Council of Basle to settle a number of hot issues of the day. A dispute over where it was heading led

Rome	Avignon	After Pisa
	Clement V (1305 – 1314) **John XXII** (1316 – 1334) **Benedict XII** (1334 – 1342) **Clement VI** (1342 – 1352) **Innocent VI** (1352 – 1362) **Urban V** (1362 – 1370) **Gregory XI** (1370 – 1378)	
Urban VI (1378 – 1389) **Boniface IX** (1389 - 1404) **Innocent VII** (1404 – 1406) **Gregory XII** (1406 – 1417)	**Clement VII** (1378 - 1394) **Benedict XIII** (1394 - 1417)	**Alexander V** (1409 – 1410) **John XXIII** (1410 – 1415)
Martin V (from 1417)		

to an attempt to dissolve it, which didn't quite work. In 1440, a rump of council members plump for the retired Duke of Savoy and make him their pope as Felix V. He gives up in 1449, ending the last schism in the Western Church, but it does the prestige of the papacy no favours.

Heresy

Well done for timing your visit to avoid the rumpus with the Templars, and their being shut down by the King of France (1307 – 1312). Albigensians from the Cathar South of France are still being burned at the stake in the late fourteenth century, but that's partly as a useful political weapon these days rather than because of huge heretical turmoil.

Still, you didn't account for the Lollards. It's said they're named because they wobble their heads. In fact they seem to have them firmly screwed on. England has mostly escaped heresy these last centuries. But with John Wycliffe, there's a reformer of the top order. A popular teacher, his work sweeps across the country.

Their beliefs include
- The primacy of the Bible
- Clergy should marry
- Indulgences, paying for the remission of sins, are wrong
- The bread and the wine is symbolic, not a miracle
- Rejecting absolution of sins
- Rejecting pilgrimage
- Opposing payment for prayers for the dead
- Clerics with posts not to double job with one from the state

Considering how radical these proposals are for the age, it is perhaps surprising that so few Lollards end up being burned at the stake over the next hundred years. Over in Bohemia, another reformer identified with Wycliffite thought, John Hus, ends up meeting precisely that fate. Hus's misfortune is not to have as powerful a set of friends to protect him, and to live at the time when the Catholic Church is settling its split. It's also partly his own fault for turning up in person at the Council of Constance as instructed and explaining his views, which the attendees turn out not to be so keen on. The King of Bohemia had expected him to get safe passage back and encouraged him to go, to get the dispute sorted out. But the stakes are, literally, high. Years of civil war follow; religious strife mostly spared the land of the Lollards.

Minority religions

Both England and France have a disgraceful history of maltreating their Jewish minorities. After centuries of failing to protect them from abuse and violence, requiring them to dress distinctly, taxing them for the privilege of following their faith, forced conversions, restricting their work and then attacking them for what financial roles are left open to them, after all that the next step is exile.

The Jews were briefly expelled from France in the late twelfth century, from Gascony in 1287, from England in 1290, and in 1306 from France.

Persecution is not uniform, but intolerance can be.

Jewish tourists are therefore unlikely to be allowed ready admission into either estate. But note that Jews are still being converted or expelled many years after these dates, so you might come across a small, hidden community.

If this is your heritage, we recommend you conceal it during your stay. You may well find enlightened individuals, especially if you have a rare skill set as, for instance, an accomplished doctor. But we suggest the last thing you want to be, when a plague breaks out, is different. Horrible as it might be, perhaps expulsion saved the following generation from a terrible fate, as the sins implied from the Black Death are clearly being visited on the right people given there's no one else around to blame.

Oriental travellers should note that there are practically no chances of encountering any Mohammedans during your stay. Paynim or pagan travellers as you are known will not have access to mosques. Most locals probably still believe moslems worship an infernal Trinity, and who is around to contradict that? On the other hand, and notwithstanding the possible encounter of the odd bar sign suggesting a decapitated Saracen, the level of outright antipathy towards muslims has dropped significantly over the past couple of hundred years. In part this has possibly been due to the congenitally angriest of locals going on crusades which they were too stupid to survive.

The next scare will be the fierce Turks. The Byzantines are pushing for a new crusade, on the grounds that their Empire is coming under severe threat as too is the territory of their neighbours. It remains to be seen what practical help the bickering powers of the West will finally supply, and whether it comes in time.

Late crusading

Crusading has been going on now for three centuries. Individually of course, as the Pope declares, participants find their sins washed away. The practical returns though have been diminishing with each expedition, and some have been outright disasters.

There have been eight major crusades so far, the last happening in 1270 which gained the French king a sainthood and an early grave. The suppression of the Templars has hindered plans for a reconquest, and the Holy Land has been completely lost. A trickle of crusaders keep up the pressure on pagans in the Baltic, until they turn Christian, and push back the Moors in Spain.

You might have signed up for a package tour to the Holy Land in 1328. Prepare to be disappointed. The start of the Hundred Years War diverts French attention from an expedition to Syria. On the plus side, that might spare you a likely death given the track record and the emergence of a new Turkish power in the region.

Another opportunity arises in the 1340s for you to go to Smyrna, on the west coast of Asia Minor. In 1363, everybody who is anybody takes the Cross, including the Kings of England and France and the Black Prince, and some opportunities exist for the more adventurous to go sailing and pillaging around large parts of the Eastern Mediterranean. Another wave of interest happens in the 1390s, and French and a few English knights go and fight in the Balkans, leading to an unfortunate defeat at the battle of Nicopolis in 1396. Church splits and fighting between countries however limits the opportunities.

Another attempt in the 1440s initially succeeds in defeating the Turks and forcing their leader to abdicate, but instead of settling for a truce the allies push on and are defeated in turn in Bulgaria.

Overall, the chances are you'll encounter a lot of people who are fired up about going on a crusade, and have even made pledges and oaths to go, but for whom it's all bad timing and inconvenient just right now.

Mont St Michel: a chance to combine pilgrimage with plunder

Pilgrimages

Pottering off on a tourist jolly of course is a different matter altogether. We mentioned the key ones earlier, but there are plenty to choose from.

One way to show off your holy credentials is to collect a pewter badge from each of the holy sites. Different places have different symbols associated with them, so for instance if you've been to Santiago, you'll buy a scallop badge on site; a trip to the Royal Chapel at Windsor might merit one of St George and the Dragon, the symbol of the chivalric Order of the Garter headquartered there and which hosts his relics; St Alban's might have a head being lopped off; a badge might also commemorate a famous person's funeral you attended, a celebrated relic or artefact, or a saint who occupies a tomb.

If travelling is your thing, leave crusading aside as that will take you to very distant and dangerous parts. Opt for the Hundred Years' War field army if your holiday is self-funding, and an itinerary of pilgrimage routes if yours is the budget approach.

Special Considerations

Embassies and consulates

There are no permanent representatives of foreign powers. The Hanse has something approaching an embassy in having a series of bases across the country as we have seen. The Popes have cardinals that might be sent on diplomatic missions, but while they also have resident ones chosen from amongst local archbishops, they might take a different world view to their papal boss and could be heavily biased. Today there are no permanent, resident ambassadors. If you find one still in town, it probably just means unfinished business dragging on.

Messages in wartime can be relayed by heralds. These enjoy immunity and are considered to verge on the neutral. Their day jobs involve running tournaments, state ceremony, and maintaining the records of which knights have which distinct design on their shields. The Marshal (from 1386, called the Earl Marshal) is the court official who runs them in England and is the person to speak to if you have any etiquette questions for a court visit.

Travellers with disabilities

People born with deformity could find themselves the subject of suspicion, since their parents may have been cursed from their association with Black Magic or evil deeds. Alternatively, you may find yourself subject to jokes in poor taste. Happily, many in the Church have taken on a more responsible and caring role.

You might find a different reaction if you have become disabled later in life, or if you have money or status. Infirmity touches all who are fortunate enough to reach old age. War injuries may evoke more sympathy, and in the case of an arm lost at Agincourt, a begging routine to fall back on in hard times (though judging from some streets, we're not sure how many limbs got left behind in that field as opposed to a threshing accident).

John of Bohemia fought at Crécy despite being practically blind. Being pointed in the right direction was not good enough and he was killed, though. We recommend aiming for pilgrim sites to pray for a cure rather than the middle of a battlefield.

Hunt, cook, eat

Wildlife

There is good hunting to be had. Wildfowl abounds. Deer roam in some numbers, though they are protected when grazing on the royal estates so be very careful where you hunt. The Normans went to all the trouble of importing fallow deer from Sicily, and their successors are just as tetchy about preserving them from poachers.

Wolves remain a threat in the countryside. If you spot a wild boar in Britain, let us know as we haven't heard of any sightings in a while. Bears haven't been seen for some hundred years now, but still roam parts of France.

In parts of Britain, especially moorland and the North, insects can be a nuisance. One handy tip to remember is the conventional wisdom that flies do not bother a horse rubbed with butter.

Whatever its cause, note that Marsh Fever (malaria) reaches as far north as the Humber, particularly along the river valleys and shorelines of the east coast. It can be a real killer during outbreaks. On a positive note, malarial fever kills syphilis so there's always an up side.

Anything that can eat you can't be good.

Monsters

Wild beasts are not the only dangers stalking the land. The traveller needs to be wary of all manner of dangerous beasts lurking in the dark woods.

Of course, it's highly unlikely you'll encounter any of these wayward critters, but forewarned is forearmed. A full inventory can be found in our companion volume, A Cautious Tourist's Bestiary: The Canterbury Tails. It suffices here to refer to a handful.

Dragons are a particular menace, as you might expect for an island one of whose people (the Welsh) use it as a national symbol, and as England has latterly adopted St George it means another's patron saint also killed one. We have heard reports on a creature in the vicinity of **Lambton** in the North East which regenerates when cut by a sword, but we have yet to witness this voracious monster for ourselves.

In the south of France, take care in the vicinity of Tarascon. There used to be a scaly beast here in Roman times that defied the greatest weapons of war. A saint pacified it but the townspeople then killed it. It is unknown whether there are any offspring awaiting to unleash vengeance.

When travelling through forests, particularly in Celtic areas, decline the hospitality of fey folk. You may find if you do so that time passes slowly in their land and on your return will catch up to you and turn you to dust. Beware of wild men of the woods, hairy fellows. Giants you can spot from a mile off, or get clues of their presence from nearby towering legumes. They are often quite civilised, but eat people and can smell the blood of local nationals. As such they are best avoided. Unicorns, by contrast, are strong but pure creatures whose horn has the power to heal. They are easily caught by commandeering a maiden and hiding nearby with a net.

Travelling by sea, or loitering near certain pools, be wary of **mermaids**. They'll enchant you and try to drag you down into the deep.

Exceedingly cautious? When you arrive at a new destination, you might check the room to see if there is a goblin resident. These are small creatures waiting to cause a nuisance in the middle of the night; but don't be spotted by your host, who might think your searching excessive. However, confirming you are imp-free means that if a nightly disturbance does take place, you'll know it's a ghost and a real menace, and that you'll need to banish it by a speedy prayer. The dead are particularly restless at certain times of the year such as Hallowe'en.

Remember that these sorts of creatures are often repelled by iron, so keep your knife with you.

Devils

Many of those monsters are now known to be associated with the underworld. The evil minions of the infernal regions, of which there are many and whose names are known to alchemists, are occasionally drawn to the land of the living to perform their nefarious demonic deeds.

We advise travellers to avoid midnight bets involving intangible parts of their being, to keep alert to the whiff of sulphur, and to carry a pinch or two of salt around with them to deploy in the wake of any quick getaway.

Don't be too quick to pet any black dogs running towards you. Indeed, best start sprinting, as they could be hell hounds. In some areas these spooky beasts are friendly but it's best not to take any chances.

Ghosts and Ghouls

England is haunted. We recommend you get hold of a copy of the Byland Chronicle as a guide to the types of spectral entities that can be found in the North of England at least. They can take the form of fearsome beasts or mobile yet normally inanimate objects, so don't be surprised if you are being chased by a rolling rock or barrel, a leaping bag of soot, or a hideous man. Occasionally the dead get up and go wandering at night until a priest can offer confession, or the body is dumped in a river. Be wary at crossroads and if your dog gets nervous.

Sorcery and wizards

Merlin may have been a heroic character, but your average sorcerer won't be. The genuine ones will have a compact with evil; the fake ones will con you out of your money while pretending to transmute iron into gold; the rubbish ones will have a six of spades hidden down their doublet.

All are trouble. Stay clear of magic for the safety of your pocket and your soul.

Culture

Music

At first sight, it may seem that you've mistimed your visit. The golden era of the songsters has gone. The minstrels known as the troubadours in the south, and trouvères in the north, are a thing of the thirteenth century and now of history.

The trade, it seems, has also professionalised. It's no longer the done thing for nobles to vaunt their poetic and singing skills by complaining about lost love, or an encounter with a foxy shepherdess -

Name that tune

at least, not outside a narrower circle. These days, popular music is a career, not a hobby.

A symbol of the change exists in the waits. These are essentially watchmen with musical instruments, typically a pipe of some description, who use them to perform such duties as highlighting their presence, the passage of time, or an uneventful watch. Over the years they become full blown musicians for hire, or part of the company of noblemen to provide regular entertainment.

The period is remarkable for an increasing number of different types of instrument. Strummed instruments include the citole, which has four strings: you might spot the Earl of Warwick amusing himself by playing with a finely carved one. There's the gittern, the lute, and the cittern too, often with local variants including differences in look and especially in the number of strings and where they sit. Tastes change over time.

Blown instruments include the flute, a large number of regional types of (bag)pipes, and the shawm (the old wait instrument). Drums make an appearance in popular beat combos. Visiting a cathedral city, track down the best of the organs.

Dancing

Different dances are appropriate for different environments. We suggest you follow the lead of your hosts. After all, you would look a bit sheepish if you attempted the new craze of morris dancing with a surprised duchess, or erroneously tried an estampie but while going around a may pole - another new big thing.

In the high and mid seasons, the main social dance across society is the carole. Hold hands and move and sing in tandem.

To be honest we have two left feet and can't tell our quadrilles from our rondels. Some are done in pairs, others lines, others again in squares. Practice makes perfect so we suggest before you go to court if that's where you're staying, get a few lessons. Out in the countryside you'll find nobody minds a misstep, so just watch a while and then join in. It's a fine way to break the ice.

Nightlife
The tavern beckons.

Shopping
Quality comes with the service in towns with a guild. Go direct to artisans' houses and do your shopping there.

You'll sometimes find clusters of tradesmen dealing with the same wares, such as shoemakers in Cordwainer Street or bakers in Bread Street. You may find St Paul's a useful stop when on the hunt for book sellers. Cheapside might be worth trying for foodstuffs. If in doubt, look for relevant street names and hope the trade hasn't moved on.

There's fun to be had amongst the cabbage stalls.

Light entertainment
Itinerant performers can brighten up your day. Settle down in front of the church, or wherever the wagons of the troupe have set up, and watch the time honoured tradition of the mystery play, and its developing cousin the morality play. Theatre, though frowned on by the Church, has been a useful tool in bringing religion to the masses in a popular and understandable way, even if the history sometimes gets skewed in the process. Comedy plays, including satire, are also beginning to develop.

If you want to be a little less static, wander around the marketplace and watch the acts on offer from a variety of artistes. There are buffoons, clowns and dwarves to make you laugh. There are acrobats and jugglers. Popular musicians play racy tunes and sing doggerels. The performers, or jongleurs, can be fluid in their skills and cut across these forms of entertainment. Don't forget to tip.

Pastimes

Sport and games

Unless you are from the Low Countries, the chances are that as a visitor to Scotland in the Low Season you will be unfamiliar with a peculiar local sport. This involves hitting a ball with a stick, the intention for it to be lost in a hole. We do not believe it will catch on.

Sundry forms of games with larger balls are certainly more broadly popular. There are a host of variants, mostly involving moving an object to one of two goal points to win. Rules vary hugely, and some are more of a scrum than others. They are typically played on a holy day and involve people from the upper end of a town or village opposing those from the other. Do feel free to muck in as it can be something of a free-for-all lasting a number of hours, often concluding with a surprise sprint after people lose sight of the ball in the mass of bodies or in the murk of nightfall. Concerns are already being raised that it risks supplanting archery as a useful pastime for the nation. You'll find bans happening in England in the 1360s.

Parents on family holidays needing a quiet moment could direct their offspring towards waifs playing the popular A le queue le leu (or 'grab the wolf's tail'). A line of children hold on to one another and the person at the head tries to catch the person at the rear.

Popular village sports include wrestling and while blindfold hitting a pig with a stick. We never said rural life was sophisticated. For the less porcinely aggressive, we suggest dice, cards or (in very high company) chess. These are somewhat frowned upon either owing to their gambling associations – which can be ruinous – or their oriental origins, but you can also plump for games such as marbles, nine men's morris, horse shoe throwing, or its original variant with hoops known as quoits. We suggest trying your arm at skittles, or nine pins, in France quilles, which involves throwing a lump of wood at other pieces of wood to knock them down. The shapes and the names change depending on the area you're in – sometimes the thrown object is a ball, and around Northamptonshire it's called a cheese as it looks like one. There might even be a distinct big skittle as well. The premise remains the same and once you know where to stand and how many throws you've got, it's an easy game to get stuck into. We think it'll make a fantastic tavern game some day.

Outdoor pursuits

There are more civilised pastimes. You can (with the landowner's permission) engage in a hunt. A pleasant ride on a fine day might also be a distraction. Falconry is another option. Hunting birds for food, such as duck, is considered very common though as it involves hiding in bushes and swamps.

The old attractions aren't dead. For the more active, attend a joust, or a tourney. Spectators are equally welcome. There's a lot to be said for watching knights in full armour bash each other, with only a moderate chance of witnessing serious wounds or death.

Great kings have menageries, and the courts of England and France are no exception. If

The best castles are beginning to have fine gardens, such as this one at Villandry.

access is permitted, go and have a look at these strange beasts, some of which have been provided as diplomatic gifts by potentates from legendary lands. Having a collection of wild exotica can also have a secondary purpose as a gladiatorial spectacle, pitting large wild cats against confused local fauna. Equally, nothing says 'Queen' quite like owning the odd leopard or occasional pet monkey.

The French in particular have a strong reputation for going out to watch events and spectacles, so be prepared for large tourist crowds when an event or parade is on.

Practical Considerations

Wills

As a foreigner you may be subject to the ius albinatus. If you die on your holiday, all your property including land belongs to the Crown. It is one reason amongst many why we do not recommend any long stay in the country unless you adopt local nationality, and a free status. On the plus side, if you're a prisoner of war, dying saves your family from ruining themselves with your ransom so there is a positive element.

However, happily if you are here for a short visit on business, or to attend one of the leading fairs of northern France, you are exempt. So the lesson is that if you are here as a pilgrim or purely for tourism, travel light and don't die.

Languages

The longer you stay in England, the more you'll notice French taking a secondary role. Introduced by the Normans as the language of the courts and of high society, it's now being supplanted by English. It's rare to see children brought up with French as their first tongue, and increasingly English Christian names are being given to nobles. In the fourteenth century there's a noted English accent when they speak French (this might be put down to it being regional Norman). But by the fifteenth century, even the country's ambassadors are speaking in bad French.

The language of Britain even then is not uniform There are very marked differences in accents, and vocabulary, that can make understanding difficult for a traveller. More strikingly, write off any casual attempt to understand Welsh, or Gaelic up in Scotland.

Differences in French are even more noted. The north and the south of country are as divided as they both are from the Catalans, Genoese, or people of Leon.

In the north there are a number of dialects of French, each significantly distinct. The language of the south however is different and not French at all. Occitan, or Provençal, evolved separately from Latin and in many ways resembles Catalan more. In the south west a slightly different evolution took place, which has led to people speaking Gascon. In each case, the local language bolsters regional identity – a fact that English kings have long recognised, ensuring in Bordeaux that locals are put in charge, whilst remembering that the old coronation oath was pronounced in neither English or French. The south is culturally, politically, militarily and for tax purposes a world apart. Ask a southerner questions about what's happening in "France" and he'll respond about a foreign country up north.

This division is best witnessed by the words the north and the south both have for 'yes'. The north says some form of 'oui', and from its spelling allows us to talk of land of the Langue d'oïl. The Provençal south has a different word for yes, which gives us the region of the Langue d'oc.

Within these regions there is further huge divergence. For example, the Normans talk of catel while the Parisians talk of chatel when discussing the mooing things, and in turn those words have turned in English into cattle and chattels. In the south, the Gascons say arriu instead of riu for river. Over time these changes have added up and it may take some time for your ear to adjust if you are travelling widely during your stay. It can also betray which side you might be on if a fight breaks out!

The other language you might just be able to make use of in an emergency, particularly if you come from further afield where don't have any French or English teachers, is (literally) the old classic. Latin is universally the language of the Church, and you can always track down a man of the cloth if you need to ask any questions. Whether he actually understands Latin, or just mouths something learned by rote, is a different matter. You can also rule out anyone understanding your Byzantine Greek too.

As time goes on, you may also hear people increasingly speaking gibberish. This is not a mark of insanity. Nor is it just that central authority has broken down and the dictatorship of the grammarians is at an end, though in some cases having lots of foreigners and outsiders in your village can introduce some strange words: an example is the slang word for an Englishman which is a "goddam".

But in fact, in many cases your overheard gabble is in fact code. It may be a special secret language known as Jargon, used in particular amongst nefarious types such as beggars, thieves and gamblers to keep their conversation secret. You can ask the poet François Villon about it when you meet him: he uses it in some of his work.

Some examples of Jargon	
Flic: an officer of the law	**Craquer la tête:** to hang
Sergot: an agent of the law	**Se plaindre:** to complain; to call out for help
Filou: a criminal	
Pitre: an unfortunate	**Ninar:** loaded dice
Vendangeur: a grape harvester; a cutpurse	**Jouet:** positively loaded dice
	Blanc: true; good
Flanquer: to imprison	**Bis:** false; bad
Devant l'instance: before the courts; under torture	**Vider:** to spend money; get rid of fakes
Faire pleurer: to put on a sob story before the judge	**Grain:** coin
Boulot: criminal work	**Droe/faux-fric/ faux-sous:** fake coin

Chapter 3
Information for Business Visitors

Red tape

Bureaucracy has yet to be quite reinvented in the style of the Roman Empire. That does not mean to say, however, that there aren't large numbers of agents of the Crown, particularly in France. Their main role half the time seems to be trying to insinuate themselves into local government, in order to wheedle things under their direct control and undermine local and ancient privileges. But as a visitor, you will hopefully avoid the consequences of this local power play.

Travellers from China may find their stay requires less paperwork. This is just as well as their ancient discovery of paper has only been picked up in western Europe in the last couple of hundred years.

Money

I don't give a groat

Currency is based on the value of the precious metal in the coin, typically silver or gold. Unfortunately, over the years a bewildering array of coins are minted of different sizes, meaning that their relative values differ.

The basic units of currency run as follows –

1 livre/**pound** (L)

=20 sous/**shillings** (s)

= 60 **groats** (in England)

= 240 deniers/**pence** (d)

= 480 oboles (in France)

=960 pites/**farthings** (or quarter pennies)

Complicating things you can also find gold coins such as the Royal, Double, Lion, Couronne and so forth. Gold coins have been in circulation in France for three generations now, but only in England from 1351.

In silver there are also such coins as the Tournois, Obole and Blanche. If in doubt, just bite it then weigh it. Worth remembering are the gold coins the Ecu d'or, worth a pound and the Franc, which arrives around 1360. There are three Marks to every two English Pounds, and yes, different mints abroad can produce different value Pounds.

The pound in your pocket

It's not so unusual to find monarchs trying to reduce the value of the coins by adding baser metals, an act called **debasement**. Some make a policy of reversing the trend by introducing a new and improved coin, a deal some call **reinforcement**. If you spot a new coin coming out, it might be worth thinking about what's in it, and what was in its predecessor. It may affect your prices. It will certainly encourage your customers to spend with the new stuff to get rid of it and hoard the old. It also contributes to Pounds being worth different amounts in different territories.

You may find it worthwhile to note that debasement happens a lot more in France than in England. The French debase, the English borrow instead. Different answers creating different problems.

In the 1330s alone the coinage gets watered down no fewer than nine times in France as each new batch of coins gets struck, and in the bad years of the 1340s the level of silver is being reduced three or even four times a year. The 1360s and the 1420s are the worst of all.

In England, apart from the 1360s and the financial dog years of the 1430s, the pound is stable. The Ecu by contrast is a very uncertain currency, a trigger for inflation, and a cause of political concern. Plus ça change...

The head of the monarch is enough to demonstrate that a coin is legal tender. But what about foreign coins you've brought with you? Providing the coins have a credible face value for their weight, you'll quite likely find them accepted at least in the ports and in London. However, when buying in bulk or selling, you can expect to be dealing with the local currency so be prepared to factor any local debasements into your sums.

The last thing you want is to find out your trading partners back home don't see the bullion value of your cash quite the same way you do, so you're ending up out of pocket when you return.

Incidentally, there are no pockets. Use a purse.

The Banking system

While Italy remains the heartland of the banking system, and the Church continues to tell people usury (or the interest on loans) is a sin, the practice has for some time now crossed the Alps. Indeed, bankers are considered an extremely useful way of providing swift loans to fill shortfalls in short term spending, like running the court while waiting for the next batch of taxes to be wheeled in.

Moneylenders are an important part of France's economy and trade, and you can find them beyond the usual big cities in places such as Cahors. But they also are a vital stopgap for many nobles, some of whom you might spot having difficulty paying up since they are spending more than they are earning. We counsel requiring payment on the nail when dealing with French barons. A lot of them are going down in the world as they parcel out their wealth to the next generation, while trying to live up to showy expectations.

Banking will provide support for the English at the start of the Hundred Years' War. But the loans will lead to a massive default. The failure by Edward III to pay up in the 1340s will contribute considerably to a crisis for the leading banking unions, the Bardi and the Peruzzi.

We would suggest avoiding the import/export market at this stage; the bankers have been given control over large parts of it to help recoup their costs, and then when things turn sour you'll find any money deposited through them could be difficult to get back.

Ironically, Edward III is the third Edward to ruin an Italian banker, since both of his predecessors had done the same too. We wonder if there's ever another King Edward if another banking family might have some troubles with their future loans.

Other measurements

On the subject of counting things out, it's not just the ratio between pounds, shillings and pence that are a little irregular to remember. There are other even more confusing measures too.

The main measurement of distance is the **mile**, a thousand paces originally. The Scottish mile is longer than the English. One eighth is a **furlong**, first intended as a ploughing measurement. In France, three miles make a **league**. At the other extreme, the English foot is slightly smaller than a French foot. We are not sure whether this is the result of bragging. Three feet make a **yard**. The **ell** measures part of all of an arm's length so that varies too. A quarter of a foot is a **hand**. A **span** is the distance between the outstretched thumb and little finger on the same hand. A twelfth of a foot is an inch, which should also be the length of three barleycorns.

An English measurement of liquid is the **gallon**. A quarter of a gallon makes up a quart. An eighth may or may not make up a **pint**. A quarter or sometimes half a pint is a **gill**.

A **ton** is the weight of a filled tun, more precisely defined with time. The **pound** varies but may have twelve ounces in it, or it may have more, depending on what is being measured. Edward III thankfully standardises it. A **mark** can be a measurement of weight or of coin, and that varies too.

The lesson is to look at what you're buying before you hand over the cash.

Guilds

Merchants and tradesmen in the area to conduct business should familiarise themselves with the local guilds system. In the absence of a strong centrally-managed economy, excepting certain key strategic industries and areas of crown monopoly, much of the regulation of key trades is carried out on a local level. Central to this, especially where towns have been given a free hand by the Crown to run their own affairs, is the guild.

Some settlements may only have a single guild, but the larger ones will often have more to look after the different interests of their groups. Membership comes by having served time as an apprentice; by being the child of a member who has taken up the trade; or by being nominated and paying your way in – this last is the route you will likely take if an outside professional who's already fully trained. Note that with whole families involved in business, women can become members in their own right, most notably widows.

You may find guilds are key centres for financing. Groups of merchants who know each other may come together to back joint trading ventures, which might include yours.

Guilds are central in setting and maintaining standards. Originally they were often covert and illegal, but now their place is recognised officially. They decide who can operate professionally (you may well have to take up membership especially if working in an area for any extended period in time). They fix prices and wages, and control working standards. They also check the quality of goods produced, which is important as they are to all intents and purposes operating a monopoly, so public confidence needs to be maintained. An example of that is prohibiting the sale of produce by candlelight, which could mask poor quality manufacture. Note that the senior people in the Guild – the Master and his Wardens – have the right to search you or your property to enforce this.

Guild membership also brings the same benefits as it did in Roman times, since it acts as a burial club. They furthermore play a charitable role in support of their members.

Some may have a strong religious flavour to them, which is not surprising given that with many members trading close to one another and sometimes congregated on the very same street, they might also form a congregation in the same local church. Before they become legal trade bodies, several existed in the form of a religious organisation celebrating saint days. Some maintain strong religious links with old Church patrons such as bodies of friars after they become recognised by the monarch.

London is a major trading centre and so you'd expect its traders to be well represented. Here you might encounter the term 'livery company' being used, which refers to the guilds' senior members having a distinctive uniform for high events. Here's a list of the various livery companies that exist locally to give you an idea of what organisations exist. The date each has been officially recognised is alongside it, though no doubt there is room for many more in the future, like bakers, cooks, ironmongers and dyers. They also give a hint as to how important the relevant trade was becoming at a moment in time. Note for instance that when those in the archery business were setting up a guild, they divided into who made the bow and who the arrow. If you undertake the work of the other, you pay a large fine.

Weavers 1155
Loriners (horse equipment) 1261
Cordwainers (leatherworkers, later shoemakers) 1272
Fishmongers 1272
Painter-Stainers 1283
Barbers (including surgeons) 1308
Armourers (later also brasiers, brass/copper workers) 1322
Blacksmiths 1325
Skinners 1327
Merchant Taylors (clothing and armour padding) 1327
Girdlers (belts) 1327
Goldsmiths 1327
Carpenters 1333
Cutlers (knives and blades) 1344
Pepperers (later, Grocers) 1345
Glovers 1349
Musicians 1350
Saddlers 1362
Drapers 1364
Vintners 1364
Plumbers 1365
Poulters (dealing in 22 kinds of poultry) 1368

Haberdashers 1371
Bowyers 1371
Fletchers 1371
Scriveners (scribes, and notaries) 1373
Pewterers 1384
Shipwrights 1387
Salters (including chemicals) 1394
Stationers (including printers) 1403
Curriers (making tanned leather pliant) 1415
Tylers & Bricklayers 1416
Brewers 1437
Leathersellers 1444

Additionally, London has a central Guildhall bringing together all its component members. One Guild leader becomes Lord Mayor and the others become aldermen for the City. You'll find similar forms of local government taking shape in guildhalls across the country, for instance in Boston, King's Lynn, and York. Norwich in comparison has nineteen guilds in 1389 and more on their way. But you'll even find them in small trading entrepots, such as tiny Lavenham in Suffolk, famous for its blue cloth. They are often interesting buildings of note and worth looking at in their own right.

You might find some tensions between the craft companies and the trade companies, so beware of that as an outsider who falls into one of those two brackets. Also note that there are borderline areas where jurisdiction is disputed between trades. In 1372, London's leather sellers catch the city's dyers colouring sheep leather to sell it as coming from deer. Scuffles are not unheard of. In 1345, hundreds die in Ghent as the weavers and fullers have a serious dispute over trade demarcation. Try to keep tabs on where your fellow traders have set up stall so you can summon some helping hands if needs be. Guilds in the Low Countries even take different sides in revolutions depending on their interests, and the splits become extremely bloody.

They often host feasts. If you get the chance, definitely attend one held by the Vintners in London, as they are amongst the rare non-royals who have rights on swans. They've had a claim on their quills and meat "since time immemorial" – which is a legal term meaning since 3 September 1189, when Richard I was crowned: a set point in time chosen by lawyers in 1275 as being beyond living memory back then. It is perhaps a measure of their status, since they have powers of search that go beyond London, and enjoy a monopoly of exports to Gascony that includes herrings and cloth as a counterpoise to their role in importing the local wine in such bulk.

Local Government

The place to be in mediaeval Europe is the free city. They are locally managed and subject to themselves.

This isn't North Germany however, and that degree of self-government doesn't quite exist over here. Still, a number of towns do have special charters allowing them some measure of self-government. These typically define the town's freedom in terms of local magnates, ensuring that the nearby lord has no say on when the tradesmen decide to hold their market, or forcing it to meet on his land and generate taxes for him. It gives them more control on how they develop the town, and frees residents from having to perform any duties as feudal dues, like military service or working on the local noble's land. Charters also might give more powers to local residents to manage some of their criminal justice system, and to levy taxes, reducing the prospect of outsider embezzlement. It might remove certain tolls altogether, thus encouraging trading in the settlement. Do note, however, that some charters are limited to trade rights so the fact a town has one might still mean it falls under some powerful figure's control.

The traders may manage their own affairs, but even with self-governance they don't get things all their own way. In the fourteenth century, the key figure is the county sheriff whose principle objective is to collect local taxes, and to maintain law and order. More places are starting to appoint or elect mayors, and elected assemblies also appear in a number of towns. Here still, power is concentrated in the hands of the wealthy rather than across the whole of the population.

Democracy is far from unfettered. The feudal system may be on the wane, but being nobility means they have wealth and still some power, especially as far as their own land is concerned. That applies to those holding church property too. Even if local Church bigwigs don't quite have unbridled control as a law totally unto themselves, the economic sway they hold means their writ flows. Nobody wants to be turfed out of their church-owned farm for messing with the abbot, after all, or finding themselves officially on a fast track to Hell.

Local legal power wanes with the increased use of Guardians of the Peace, and later Justices of the Peace, who are centrally appointed with a writ covering the whole land. Their introduction is slowly overturning the old anglo-saxon methods of communal responsibility for helping neighbours fight crime.

In France, if anything these differences are exaggerated. There is the king's writ running over the royal domains; certain highly urban areas particularly in the far north and south jealously striving to guard their privileges and trading interests; and the great dukes pushing their own landed interests in the regions.

Perhaps the nearest we can see of this strange mix in England is in Durham. This is run by a Prince-Bishop who has a crucial historical role in guarding the area against the Scots. This important vice regent had his own taxation powers, his own army, his own coins, his own local government, and even his own small parliament.

This leads to a peculiar situation where Durham sends no MPs to Westminster, but Calais does.

National Government

High politics will scarcely be of concern for the tourist, but a brief note may be of value.

Central government is centred ultimately on the King. There are checks and balances, which are more informal in France, and increasingly set out in England following on from the basic principles of the **Magna Carta** (especially its provision that taxation must be by consent).

In England, Parliament unites a lower chamber for the non-nobility, with an upper called the House of Lords, and the person of the Sovereign. Membership of the former is determined by election, and thanks to Edward III has recently taken new form. The knights of the shires, two representing each of thirty seven counties, and 222 delegates from the towns, have sat together jointly since 1332, and separately from the Lords and from the King since 1341.

All freemen have the right to vote. From 1429, after a number of poor people end up being elected, the vote is restricted to people owning (not renting) forty shillings' worth of land. Note, however, that though this limit won't be removed, the threshold needed equally won't be increased, meaning the number of qualifying voters will grow by itself over time thanks to the effects of inflation.

Parliament meets in the Chapter House of Westminster Abbey from 1352, and from 1397 in its refectory (mind the half-eaten chickens if you're there to watch). The law courts over in the old Norman Westminster Hall are usefully opposite.

The King has also resolved that Parliament should meet annually, creating a regular forum for discussion. With a secure footing established, you will note the Commons gaining in confidence over time. It elects its first spokesman, Sir Peter de la Mare, in 1376. His successor, Thomas Hungerford, the following year is first credited with the title of Speaker.

Two will become a little too confident. In 1399, Sir John Bussy will be beheaded after an ungainly and excessively profitable career removing opponents of Richard II. William Tresham ends up murdered in 1450. We have no doubt more will follow thanks to the civil wars to come – we don't fancy Tresham's son's chances much for instance.

The House of Lords meanwhile consist of two groups – the Lords Spiritual, and the Lords Temporal. The former are the two archbishops, score or so of bishops, and a small number of abbots. The latter are the various peers of the realm, though only perhaps one in three turns up so the place is never too crowded.

But with Edward III's changes, watch the House of Commons from now on. The 1376 Parliament gains the title of the **Good Parliament**, as the Commons impeaches a number of corrupt ministers. The 1386 goes one better and gets the title of the **Wonderful Parliament**, as it manages to get the Lord Chancellor dismissed and impeached as well. The **Merciless Parliament** in 1399 on the other hand deposes the king, Richard II. They are rather ruthless in their actions and can take shortcuts in dealing out justice.

Compare this with the system as it is developing in France. The country is run from Paris, which has its own **Parlement**. Over time, more local parlements are added to areas long enjoying some degree of local character and independence, starting with the south of the country and then more as new territories are added to direct crown control. Ironically, the more of France falls into the hands of the French king, the more divided the kingdom becomes between those areas traditionally under his control, and those where new subjects are allowed a measure of self-governance in order to keep them from rebelling against the changed political order. It's not difficult to predict that giving both these privileges and the means to defend them will have long term effects if reforms are ever needed in the distant future, especially of the bizarrely unfair tax system.

The French monarch can also summon an **Estates General** uniting the three classes of the realm – the First Estate or clergy, the Second Estate being the nobility, and the third drawn from everyone left over (the majority). This happens rarely; the main players amongst the first two are often seen at court anyway, and every time they are summoned they tend to want something that limits the king's power. Still, you may bump into people summoned to attend one, as several do get called, particularly when taxes are needed or once a French king gets captured. The results can be counterproductive and in the latter part of the fourteenth century they actually trigger revolts. Charles VII learns from this – once they finally give him the go-ahead to raise money, he considers it a general permission to do so without ever bothering them again. As representative government goes it's far from exemplary. If Parlements won't fix future problems, the Estates General will one day make them worse. But that's a Hundred Years' War legacy that will be for a future French monarch to discover.

Taxation

If you happen to be a merchant, you'll obviously have a strong interest in how the taxation system works. You'll have to pay up at some point after all. So here's a very brief introduction for you.

Tenths and **fifteenths** are "fractional taxes", levying a rate that is a specified fraction of the individual's (moveable) wealth. These are the most frequent fractions but you might hear of others, and it's possible you encounter multiples. The rate is set nationally but local collection can be tweaked to suit people's known individual ability to pay.

This method is used to tax imports and exports except wine. There, **prisage** used to take one tun (or great barrel) of wine for every ship importing ten or more, and two for every ship importing over twenty. That has now changed since the start of the fourteenth century. **Butlerage** applies to foreign merchants for a two shilling tax per imported tun. As a foreign merchant, you're also set to pay a surtax on your goods that your English competitors won't, but they'll likely have to face your situation when trading as a foreigner in your home town. Unless you plan to settle down, you'll probably avoid the other fiscal burdens. The **poll tax** is levied on any individual over a certain age, rather than assessed on property. Some people are exempt.

If you come across something called a **subsidy**, it means a tax on either the income from your land, or on moveable goods, whichever is more.

A **forced loan** is where the king's soldiers encourage you to volunteer some money into his coffers. You may or may not see it back – if not, they are called **benevolences**.

Note that the Cinque Ports (q.v) in the south avoid paying land taxes as they provide direct support to defend the realm, a **ship tax**, but being based there won't make you immune from some of the other taxes. As a foreigner, or **aubain**, you may in France have to pay a tax if you marry a local national. There may be an annual flat tax for simple residency too. You will be exempt if your stay is short and on business.

You might encounter **bonds** as an importer. These are deposits to ensure people keep to the terms of a contract, in this case if you cannot pay customs dues immediately. You will get the money back if the terms are kept. Bonds may also be used potentially by a greedy monarch as a tool for bribery to sway his judgement.

Recognisances are acknowledgement by the king, especially a new king, that former royal debts are still valid. They are also possibly open to abuse.

It's unlikely you'll encounter them as it mostly affects wards, and unmarried heiresses, but there's also royal money to be made in **feudal dues** where the Crown looks after the interests of orphans (at a price). Everybody wants to marry a rich young lady who owns a castle, after all.

There is also taxation levied by the clergy. This is in tenths, and is called the **tithe**. It's often paid in kind, that is to say not in coin but in produce. The ancient tradition of paying **Peter's Pence**, a penny donation, is however largely out of practice (when not kept by bishops for themselves) and stopped by Edward III. The clergy themselves run their own tax affairs, which may or may not be used to support the monarch.

Taxation on individuals happens infrequently, and tends to happen when specifically needed – most notably, when a war is about to start or a revolt is in the offing. Taxes might also be forthcoming if there are special court events, such as the knighting of the heir, or the marriage of the king's eldest daughter. Note that this should only apply to those owing feudal duties to the monarch, and even then only direct vassals, so if a tax collector tries to make you pay these, refuse to cough up and complain to the guild.

From 1353, you'll see the establishment of what are known as the **Staple** towns or ports. These are the authorised places for trading in wool, leather and lead. The places in question are Newcastle-upon-Tyne, York, Lincoln, Norwich, Westminster, Canterbury, Chichester, Winchester, Exeter, and Bristol; for Wales at Carmarthen; and for Ireland at Dublin, Waterford, Cork, and Drogheda. Calais is later added and becomes a key venue. These are the only places where importing and exporting these goods can take place, and there are courts set up to cover trade disputes. The idea is to secure Crown control over the market and to increase English tax revenue, since the trading venues had previously been closer to the cloth manufacturers over in the Low Countries themselves.

When paying taxes, make sure you keep a receipt. This will take the form of a **tally stick**. This is a small strip of wood with notches cut into it. The amount paid is represented by the width of the notches cut. £1,000 is a palm width (let's hope you're not paying that); £100 a thumb width; £20 the little finger; £1 the width of a swollen barleycorn; a shilling is a line thinner than a penny. Once the marks are made, the wood is split along its length, and the owner's details written down. The taxman takes the shorter piece, the taxpayer the longer. That way both sides have a record.

In England's territories many of the same principles come to apply. Taxation is an important area of dispute, and indeed it helps trigger the second part of the wars when two arguing lords appeal to the King of France rather than to their immediate overlord the Duke of Gascony to settle a tax dispute. Note however that in the south west taxation is highly devolved, at least in peacetime. If you're lucky, you might find that a settlement deal is being pushed to get loyal subjects to move out there, and if you can claim an affinity with England you might be in with a chance to get a tax break, pardon or possibly land. The down side is that you can expect to sign up to military service to defend your new homeland, and it is something of a longer term deal than many travellers will want to commit to. But in terms of your taxed goods, in Bordeaux you should look at the terms of the grand **coutume**. This is the set of terms for the export tariffs, particularly with regard to wine. A small number of the big towns and their residents are exempt, resulting in competitive street prices in England. The protectionist arrangement also hinders wine merchants from further east from bringing their produce in before a certain date, making them miss the prime market prices.

Generally across France, levied taxation is typically achieved through the **tailles**. These are set amounts, left to the local authorities to decide how best to raise amongst their taxpayers. The poor might for example pay a poll tax and the richer a lesser or greater share of their wealth. In the south, this often takes the form of the **hearth tax**, as opposed to the north which prefers to tax movables and personal wealth. England has been moving away from **tallage**, which can be arbitrary, into more closely defined rates.

There is also the **aide**, or sales tax, often triggered as in England by a special event at court or a war, but in any event happening irregularly.

Customs duties are also levied of course on the French side.

More unpopular is the **gabelle**. Initially a sales tax, from 1360 it becomes permanent, and it is increasingly associated with the duties raised on the royal monopoly of that basic necessity, salt. However, it's a working man's tax as the upper orders often find themselves exempted. The worst part is that over time the tax becomes skewed with some areas paying vastly more than others. Of course, self-interest will block reform.

In different areas, more or less emphasis could be placed on different forms of taxation to raise the required amount, so some towns could opt for a fixed fractional tax that brings in the sum. Transparency in the system means that people are assessed and reveal their wealth, and that other people can challenge the assessment if they think there's a cover up.

The **champart** meanwhile is a personal arrangement (which might include crown lands) whereby a tenant pays rent as a share of produce.

Those are a lot of ways to force you to pay money. How bad does taxation get? It's telling that the wine tax Charles VII introduces begins at one hundredth and ends as a quarter. Factor it into your profit margins.

Trade

So what wares should you be loading your cog up with when you come visiting these fine parts, and take with you on your way back? Here are some of our recommendations

Wool

Wool is an important part of England's economic life. The fact is commemorated when, in Edward III's time, the Lord Chancellor begins to sit on the woolsack when presiding over the House of Lords. It's also Edward III who encourages Flemish weavers to settle in the country to build up the indigenous cloth making industry.

Sheep breeds vary. In the North West and South West, rugged types prevail. In the East, the sheep are longhaired and the wool is of a different quality: rough edges of the fibres mean they cling better to one another, resulting in a lightweight fabric that should shrink less after getting wet. Some suggest that the difference is due to there being slower rivers in the east; others, that riverside plots are more expensive, both meaning fewer opportunities to use watermills to power the fulling process for short haired fleeces. Whatever the reality, you'll note that the industry has spread into many smaller communities now with cloth makers even set up in conveniently-sited villages. You have no excuse as you go about your travels for not spotting some exquisite fabrics that will make great presents for friends and family back home, who'll appreciate your gift on a cold winter's night.

Herring

Lampreys may be the fish of choice for the rich, but it's herring that marks out the east coast of England as a principality of the palate. Everybody on the continent knows the best come from Yarmouth. Salted, smoked or pickled, a few barrels of these will go down well when exported to an inland town on the continent. Other fish are also in the North Sea in abundance, and grow to immense size.

Stained glass

England and France produce excellent examples of stained glass, which are particularly useful for making windows to keep bats out of churches. However, it is fragile and difficult to export.

That applies doubly for the beautiful and intricate glassware blown for the table of princes.

Coal

Rather than bring your fuel all the way from Burgundy, ship it over from England. The material has been known locally since Roman times.

Metal

England has been exporting lead and tin for thousands of years. Iron is another option.

Alabasters

A centre for excellence for carving church madonnas out of alabaster emerges in the Midlands town of Nottingham. They are very popular in Aquitaine, and increasingly capture the imagination of architects in Normandy.

It's not as random an industry to find as you might think. The stone is found in the neighbourhood. The artisans can also put their hand to good altar pieces too. The white lustre of the stone renders the results aesthetically pleasing and symbolically pure. The softness of the stone helps make carving go quicker and more easily. Keep your eyes open for the workshops of Coventry, Burton, York, Lincoln and London, as there are artisans working there also.

Enamels

Limoges is a famous centre for enamels. Previously, its main market has been in what's called the champlevé style, meaning the glass has been poured into metal spaces, often copper but possibly a richer metal. Its rich blues and golden figures in particular stand out. Increasingly these days though a new technique is being used, adding monochrome painting.

Either way, the end result is a beautiful and often practical artwork. Do you have a relic at home that just gets lost on the table amongst your documents? Then what you need is a special reliquary so the holy bone doesn't roll away.

Pottery

The ceramics of the era are peculiar, jaunty and fun. Often glazed, they have a shiny lucre even if occasionally they can be a bit gaudy to the civilised eye. Try out shelly ware for a rough and ready look. Check out the green glaze pots from Nottingham if you are an earlier traveller, or the peachier versions later on. Alternatively, dip into a pile of gritty wares and sandy wares. In the north, look for the Humber ware, and the white ware from Surrey in the south. That's just some of what's in England: the point is there's a lot of choice and a market that's open to all tastes.

Ceramics

Aside from the pottery, England is beginning to get a reputation in its own right as a production site for quality tiles, good enough to use in royal palaces.

Stone

Stone from Purbeck resembles the ancient imperial marble known as Porphyry, but comes at a fraction of the diplomatic and economic cost.

Gold/silverware

Don't get too attached to items made of these precious metals. Anything less than exquisite always runs the risk of being treated as plate, that is to say considered most important for the intrinsic value of the metal, and melted down to pay soldiers and creditors. Still, jewellery has its place and its buyers.

Tapestries

Nobody likes living in a dull house. Rather than live in cold bleak rooms, invest in a tapestry or two. Despite their bulk, they have the advantage of being portable, as they are meant to travel with the noble as he visits his several estates, so bringing them back home shouldn't be impossible. In particular if you are around northern France, enquire if the town you are staying at has any reputable tapestry makers.

There are several good examples in private collections to inspire your purchase. Look out for the Devonshire Hunting Tapestries as an example of the colourful and action packed designs you can find on the market, for a price. You can find them in England at the end of the Low Season. They've probably come over from Arras or Tournai, and give a wonderful idea of what life is normally like outside if you are confined indoors by the rain. Other favourites include courtly scenes, outdoors life and work, life as a knight, mythological beasts, and biblical or historical events. Visiting Angers, look for the Apocalypse Tapestry, which is a massive undertaking for the Duke on a religious theme.

Wines

By the end of the Hundred Years' War, around a third of all of England's imports consists of wine. Of course, it helps if as monarch you happen to own some of the finest vineyards in the world. It also helps if Gascon merchants get such excellent trading concessions from the Crown. Don't expect such perks as an outsider.

The most favoured is the red, or claret. Beyond English reach, Gaillac's wine (north east of Toulouse) enjoys a strong reputation. Burgundian wines also sell well. If you get some from Champagne, check first to see that it's pale and still as on rare occasion some dreadful bubbles may sneak into the process and ruin the taste.

Do remember that wines have a short lifespan and should be consumed within a year or so owing to the storage process, since they are kept in great barrels.

Artwork

Your campaigning might take you across the Low Countries, and into the halls of wealthy burghers and nobles. If so, keep an eye open for a spot of portable plunder on the walls.

At the outset, the Gothic style of painting is flourishing, but a new form of realism is beginning to seep in from Italy. The works of Jan van Eyck are a particular treat. You can find him in Bruges and Lille in the second half of the 1420s and might commission a portrait from him there. His work is impressively naturalistic and his portraits impossibly lifelike, bringing the miraculous techniques of Italy to northern Europe. Watch him working you can see part of his secret – rather than using colours bound by eggs, he's using oil paint.

Van Eyck's great contemporary is Robert Campin, and you can find him at Tournai. It's said you can find something of the Burgundian sculpture in his portrait lines, but a measure of the detail is the way he gets people's eyes to catch the light. Campin's apprentice is Rogier van der Weyden, and if we personally admire his handling of the light less, his technical detail in creating scenes rather than focused portraiture demonstrates real skill and leadership amongst his contemporaries.

Alternatively, you could plump for some religious art. The Wilton Diptych is a fine portable altarpiece owned by Richard II, full of gold and rich blue and showing the three kings and a parade of angels with the Madonna and child. It gives us an exquisite example of private and readily transportable religious art.

Weapons

This being a warzone, you should find plenty of opportunities to trade in military equipment, or just buy the odd defensive tool for your own protection. There's always Christmas to consider - why not pick up some second hand spoils of war on the market for a song?

An old favourite in English markets is the falchion, which is a sword with a sturdy hacking blade. Axes are still occasionally in use, including by

monarchs, but nowhere near as common as in anglo-saxon days. Throwing things these days is just uncouth. If you do want a missile weapon, then your obvious choice in Britain is the bow. The longbow is swiftly developing a reputation as the revolutionary weapon on the fourteenth century battlefield: fast, mostly reliable (except in very wet weather), but above all a powerful tool for punching through armour. It's a social leveller in the process. Now, any old peasant from the hills has the ability to kill his social betters almost from beyond shouting distance, no matter how much gold his lordship forks out on the best armour available.

One-on-one with an archer, you're in trouble when you get much closer than around a hundred yards, but in a battle a mass volley becomes an issue at perhaps two hundred and fifty. Add some rudimentary protection like a wall of stakes or a battlement and you can see the defensive implications.

A new revolution helps turn the tables on the French side in the following century. Although the English perhaps first tentatively use it in battle and also in a siege, it is the French who grasp the importance of developments in artillery. Jean Bureau, the real victor at Castillon, was Charles VII's Master Gunner and both he and his brother were involved in the deployment of cannon. The sound of the artillery was also what drew the crucial reinforcements in to defeat the English at Formigny in Normandy. It's perhaps no quirk that cannons feature in both the crucial battles that close the mediaeval period, since they also play a vital role in the fall of Constantinople.

But export is not the same as expert. They are tricky and fickle beasts. We have bad feelings about James II of Scotland's fortunes and would advise not to stand too close to either him or his favourite piece when it's being lit. Best leave it to the professionals.

Stick to trading in armour. Rich people need it; rich people have money.

Armour too is going through a period of invention and revolution. The old clunky stuff, with a layer of chainmail plugging up the gaps between the metal, is out. With armour coming in so many pieces, it's important though to know your culet from your couter.

Let's start at the top. There are many different types of helmet on the market. Moving away from the common old **pot**, the simplest is perhaps the **kettle hat**. One common type is the **basinet**, which is open at the front but protected round the sides and top. You can get visors as extras. If it's too heavy, try a lighter style called the **salade**. Don't neglect investing in some fine head gear as nothing sells a suit of armour like a bright crest or some weird mythical beast model clinging to the summit.

Across the top of these, you can offer a model that carries a **comb** or spine that adds extra strength. Huge helmets, which become less popular with time, have space for small metal **coiffes** or caps to fit underneath and add some more protection. The gaps in the front are styled the **occularium**.

Now, it may be that the helmet doesn't protect the neck. One option is to add an **aventail**, a strip of chain mail that drapes down. If the face is the problem, then suggest the **bavier**, which protects the lower part and throat. A separate piece can cover the remainder of the front.

For the main part of the body there's obviously the breast and back plate. The **fauld** extends the armour by strips down over the abdomen. The **plackart** increases the protection at the front.

Practice makes perfect in Bury.
Artist: Graham Sumner, (c) Bury Council Museums Service (see later on visiting Bury)

There are all manner of bits and bobs to provide localised protection on the upper torso. There's the **besage** that protects the armpit, or if chainmail the **gusset**. **Munnions** can cover the shoulders across the top, or if you are after something more substantial plump for the **pauldron**. **Couters** defend the elbow and the **vambrace** the lower arm. **Rerebraces** can then supplement both. **Gauntlets** cover the hands. Joints can be further protected by having plates jut out excessively. A number of specialised bolt-ons provide added protection for the jousting arena which we won't cover here.

Downstairs, don't forget to offer some form of armoured codpiece. The **culet** meanwhile protects the posterior.

Down on the legs, offer the client a set of **chausses** if he likes old style chain mail. If solid metal, go for **cuisses** for the thighs, and **greaves** for the shins. Cover your joints with metal knee caps called **poleyns**, and your feet with **sabatons**. Any gaps between the midriff and the leg protection can be covered by hanging down a **tasset**.

But wearing metal without anything between it and you when it's been walloped is not a good idea either. That's why the customer needs to buy an **aketon** to act as padding underneath the armour too. Padding can also be worn over the armour in the form of the **jupon**, which is an easy way of displaying your coat of arms.

That's quite a selection of items so your profit margin is quite agreeable already. Add to these a decent shield, plus all the armour and protection the knight's horse also needs, and you are looking at a tidy trade. Just remember to scratch off any chivalric heraldry from the poor sap who was last wearing it before the unfortunate incident with the longbow. And also remember that pomp for the leaders rather than a full effective armoury is more important early on: getting absolutely everybody equipped to the hilt is a concern for later years.

Monopolies

You may find that ownership of key assets creates a local monopoly, either in practice or in law. An example is that of the village windmill and the grinding of corn, and from that the baking of bread. On the island of Sark for instance, feudal rights include a monopoly on pigeons, marriage, and also confirmation of land sales – it's a situation we logically can't see lasting much longer into the enlightened fifteenth century. But be aware of local feudal rights as they may limit what you are permitted to do and sell.

Even where there is no monopoly, be aware that export licenses might be required, obviously associated with a cost. An additional risk at times of financial difficulty is that of appropriation: the Crown might force you to sell your goods in a process known as **purveyance**, and the rate paid might be at their value, below it, or even on credit. The idea is that the material is used to plug gaps in supplying the army or the royal household, but a corrupt official might simply sell the stock on and keep the profit. *Your* profit.

The Hanse

A separate dynamic in trade comes thanks to the existence of the Hanseatic League. This is a trading association based in the Baltic but stretching out into the North Sea.

German merchants from Hanse towns form an important and privileged community in England, and testify to the trading links that exist. In many coastal ports, the Hanse has acquired trading privileges allowing for special access to the local markets, property rights, and monopoly powers in the Baltic. One noted trading centre is in London, at the Steelyard. Raw goods such as grain, furs and timber are brought over, and cloth and finished goods transported back. The alliance between Hanse towns is informal, somewhat unlike the precise privileges levered from their western trading associates.

In short, the monopoly and special rights are great if you a German traveller, but be prepared for some possible grief from locals. Thanks to the Hanse's role in acting as bankers for the English on the outbreak of war, they also now enjoy a dominant and one-sided role in shipping wool overseas – a fact that local merchants are none too happy about.

Chapter 4
The War Itself

Mercenary work

No work visa is required. There are good opportunities for employment with the French during this period, particularly if you are a crossbowman. However, do not expect to be treated with the fullest respect you deserve, particularly if you are standing between an impatient knight's horse and the English.

Freelancing offers excellent opportunities after the Battle of Poitiers for a good half century onwards. We recommend identifying a mercenary band and tying in your lot with them. You'll probably get better pay and conditions. In the south the brigandage comes across as more organised and structured, often including freelancing Gascons and English but anyone can have a go. In the east by the 1430s, the marauders are called the **Skinners**, and these French thugs are a different order of nasty.

As a freebooter, so long as you're affiliated with one of the two warring sides, if you make a deal on raising ransom from a community or just from a captive's family, the law is actually on your side. A deal struck is a binding contract, even if made under duress, and treated as such by the law and by the people who maintain it. However, that won't always stop an angry lynch mob of locals from taking matters into their own hands if they get the chance.

On the other hand, being associated with a particular knight may be safer for your long term health. If caught as a freebooter, and especially if caught associated with a weapon that's lethal to knights like a gun, you might be treated as outwith the rules of war and butchered. This makes it all the more important to confirm which side you're approaching in poor light - assuming the ruffians actually have a side.

Look out for the standards first of all, while remembering the English standard has just acquired 'quarters' of the royal French lilies on a blue background. You might in the night or in limited visibility have to rely on sound. Joining a scrap in the mist, remember that the war cry of the Gascons is the name of their province, "Guyenne", possibly adding the English favourite of a reference to St George. Having a famous commander in the field can mean soldiers yelling out his name. The French shout out their patron's name, St Denis, or their ancient cry of "Montjoie" (said to refer to a mountain outside of Jerusalem).

A Pillaging Rulebook

1. Pick your company. Early on, you'll find the English, Bretons and Navarrese (rather far from home) running around the north west, Gascons around the south, and Flemish and English in the north east. Later, you'll find French bandits in the east, English and Gascons in the south west, and English in the north and west. So second languages are useful.

2. Raid deep. Places on the frontier have probably been pillaged a lot. Easier and richer pickings can be found further away. War-torn communities also tend to build and maintain walls.

3. Capture a strong point through a surprise night assault, then use it to terrorise the locals. The aim is to capture people you can ransom, ransack the area for moveable wealth, get paid protection money to stop running rampant, then get paid out and move on. The best part is that pay-off agreements are recognised in law.

4. Remember that contracts hold but the rules of war are fluid. Monks and nobles are fair game for bandits. Some of your colleagues torture and kill and commit horrible acts so you may need a strong stomach. You may find in such company the locals (quite understandably) aren't forgiving if they catch you, despite agreements you've made with their social betters.

5. Keep in contact. You'll raid in small groups under a leader; you stand more of a chance though if you can come together to create a short-term small army if the locals get organised.

6. Bribery works. Whether it's someone looking after a castle gate or a late night sentry, and especially if they are a mercenary from the same country as you, silver offers a way in. Remember too that some locals will find room for profit in trading in the profits of your nefarious activity.

7. Ceasefires are for sissies. No matter if the King of England has agreed a truce with the King of France, there's profit still to be had by local raiding.

8. Choose your timing. The best opportunities come when central government has collapsed, such as when the King is captured; when there's social disorder like a revolt; or major nobles are going their own way. As long as you have local towns spending on defences rather than paying central taxes or contributing to armies, you've got a free run in the field.

9. Aim for centrally-managed regions, where royal power is strong. Because when he's gone, there's no one left to take command.

10. Pick a cover name, like "the Archpriest". It sounds cool, and might be helpful for later alibis.

Knights to See You, to See You, Knights

The upper classes are still driven by the rules of knighthood, which at least govern how they should treat each other in and after fighting, even if armed peasants may be fairer game. Since there is no uniform international law on war, this is rather handy for when important personages fall into enemy hands, and this happens a lot.

Essentially, it means that when cornered knights are permitted to surrender. Captured knights are held to ransom, though treated according to their rank while in captivity. This assumes the captive is securely held. If as at Agincourt there's a danger of prisoners being rescued and put back into the fray, the rules might be bent and prisoners executed. Practicalities trump niceties. Even so, the English and French have a better reputation than the Germans with their prisoners; these latter are said to hold theirs in terrible conditions, and

Death comes in shiny packages.

to demand unreasonable and utterly ruinous ransoms every time. A good trick can be to invite a knight to state his own ransom, as he won't want to downplay his worth.

There are courts to review some aspects of warfare. Admiralty courts can review challenges of naval "prizes", literally things that are taken, especially where third party nationals are involved. But in many cases it is a case of finders keepers, or clobberers nickers. Plunder is an accepted part of the process, indeed a key part of the recruitment appeal. You shouldn't rob churches though, and violence against ordinary folk who have surrendered with a city is bad form if they clearly had nothing to do with the place holding out. A troublesome garrison or community leader who declined surrender when he had ample chance, and held your schedule up, is probably fair game though.

If you are playing by the rules, some other key points to note are as follows;

- Ownership of territory can be settled by right of conquest
- Only just wars should be fought
- Neutrality should be recognised, but you can pass through their lands to get to your enemy
- Unarmed priests, and women, should be immune from violence

- Houses should not be burned
- Agreements can be made for sieges to conclude peacefully if the besieged are not relieved after an agreed period in time
- Rules for a campaign should be set out in the army's ordinances. Check these out to remove any doubt on your rules of engagement
- The punishment for such breaches of discipline includes the death penalty

Papal attempts to ban crossbows and archery in combat against Christians (Article XXIX of the Second Lateran Council) have long been ignored. Don't listen to people who want to stop you raising a quarrel. It'll probably be a worried knight who's complaining while coming at you.

These conventions don't mean bad things don't happen. Even early on you'll come across churches burnt with people inside them. It tends to be when fighting has been unexpectedly tough that the victors take it out on anybody nearby. Some combatants such as the Bishop of Tournai are clergymen but are also partisan and who own real estate with soldiers, so abbeys in their lands could well end up being plundered. As fighting goes on, the niceties soon get forgotten. In 1346, the citizens of Thérouanne are led out of town by their bishop, but are still massacred by the invading army.

Freebooting soldiers meanwhile often live completely outside of morality, living a life of plunder and worse. They fall between jurisdictions, yet are protected by the law whenever contractual agreements are made to pay them to go away. As early as 1364 these groups get excommunicated by the Pope, and indulgences provided to pardon the sins of those who die fighting them. That doesn't work, so a scheme is cleverly put together to offload them onto a Crusade and kill two birds with one stone. This unhappily fails when the concerned locals in Strasbourg refuse to let them wander across their lands, quite reasonably. They are then pointed in the direction of the Moors in Spain, leading to their triggering a civil war in a Christian kingdom there. If you're a daring mercenary with a sense of dash, France is certainly a land of opportunity for you.

For those following the code of honour though, chivalry has its down side. If invited to join the **Order of the Star** by John II, don't accept. Part of the conditions is that you are not allowed to run away. This results in most members dying horribly on the battlefield in the 1350s or being captured like the King. In any case it's only a less-exclusive mimic of the **Order of the Garter**, which Edward II has set up in 1347 and which we think has more long-term staying power.

Chivalry occasionally drives knights into ridiculous vows. On one embassy to Flanders, several English knights wander around with eye patches which they had pledged not to remove until they had accomplished some feat of valour. At the other extreme, Sir Robert Ferrers borrowed a rowing boat and practically single-handedly took on a castle: its commander thought an army was behind his tiny party and surrendered.

The key lesson is to be clear about what minimum standards you are expected to maintain, and to try to take a nobleman alive for ransom. It could finance your entire holiday, if not your life.

Our top ten battles

Bludgeoning types will not be disappointed by the thunder of hooves and flash of steel. Given the number of sieges and scraps going on, you'll need to pick your battles with care in order to avoid disappointment. Nobody wants to turn up to a muddy field to witness a rained-off no-show, or hang around for a siege going nowhere over several dysentery-filled months. So here's our pick of the best.

(1)   Sluys 1340

The situation: Sluys is the major port in Flanders and a large draw for merchantmen and warships alike. A huge French fleet has been gathering in the harbour in anticipation of an invasion of England. The English now intend to link up with their allies in Flanders. The French decide to take a defensive position and chain their ships together in three main lines.

The battle: Edward barges his way into the port. Several English ships are lost in the hand to hand fighting, but his fleet smashes through the French lines, and some help comes from supporters on shore who weigh into the French from their side. Edward is wounded by a bolt, but he recovers. The blow to the French and to their fleet is more enduring.

Top tips: English archers have a superiority in speed over their crossbow-armed opponents, so make the most of their covering fire. English knights also have over the past few years been fighting dismounted a lot more than their counterparts so that should be an advantage too. Remember though to judge your distances very carefully. It's no use capturing a vessel with all the ransom that comes with it, only to misjudge your step when leaping onto the next. Men in armour don't float.

(2)   Crécy 1346

The situation: Sluys led to a campaign of pottering around French-held towns in the north but no lasting gain. Edward III wants a real success. He lands in Normandy, and breaks through French positions into the French north. The English have travelled substantially but have had the benefit of some rest. The French are eager to deploy.

The battle: The English (and Welsh) deploy in strong defensive positions, making use of the local terrain, to which they add the crucial addition of basic field defences - ditches. Their knights are dismounted, their archers positioned to enfilade the attackers and fire on their flanks. The Genoese crossbowmen advance but are hindered by having wet weapons from a thunderstorm. The English archers pull out their dry weapons and decimate the Genoese. The impatient French knights ride through and over the retreating crossbowmen ('falling on top of one another like a litter of piglets'), but in turn become disordered as volley after volley of arrows rain down on them. The battle is an utter disaster for the French. John, Count of Luxembourg and King of Bohemia, despite being practically blind, is just one of those at the forefront where he and his companions are slain.

Top tips: It shouldn't be too difficult to survive this one. There's some hard fighting around the Prince of Wales, as Edward III wants to make him prove himself, which he does. If you want an easier life find another part of the line.

There's more fighting, and easy pickings, the next day as English forces bump into leaderless groups wandering the field in the mist, and confused reinforcements.

If you're a late visitor you won't see much other than some open fields. You'll need an aerial view. Try to grandstand from the windmill, which was where Edward had his headquarters.

(3)   Calais 1346

The situation: Crécy has opened up possibilities of major conquest. Edward's eye is drawn to the fortified port of Calais, which offers real opportunities as a key base both militarily and as a trading outpost.

The battle: There are a couple of attempts to storm the walls, but this is mostly a siege. This is, after all, one of France's strongest frontier towns. A major French relief column approaches towards the end, but thanks to unfavourable approaches declines the battle to relieve the city.

Top tips: Settle down and bring along such home comforts as you can. This one will last a year, and it's a waiting game. There'll be more sieges in later years, this time by the French and with less success. On the plus side, the whole city and all its contents fall into English hands so there's a great opportunity for loot, or even to grab a holiday home for your own. But duck offers during quiet siege time to go off on local forays, as some of these don't turn out very well.

(4)   Neville's Cross 1346

The situation: It's not just the French front which is active this year. In autumn, David II invades the north of England to distract the English after their successes across the Channel. Obviously, the northern barons don't take this lying down, and gather their forces to repel them.

The battle: It's difficult to count these things, but it looks like there's a larger Scottish force. The battle is touch-and-go for some while. However, the English have had the opportunity to pick the ground, and this will tell. With their flanks protected by steep slopes, and the Scots' advance broken up by scattered ditches, by the time the invaders' line makes contact it is disorganised and peppered. The English right flank is pushed back, but the arrival of cavalry reserves turns fortunes. The other Scottish flank then gives way. That leaves King David and his centre being wrapped round on both sides. The remainder of the Scots flee, and the King is captured.

Top tips: Given the choice, plump for the left flank and you should have a fairly straightforward battle. There's quite a bit of fighting and chasing that follows so keep some energy in reserve for the pursuit – a fresh horse might be useful.

(5)   Poitiers 1356

The situation: Prince Edward has launched a campaign in the south west. Last year, he reached as far as Carcassonne, taking the lower city but failing against the ancient and sturdy twin walls of the main fortifications. An expedition in Normandy has retreated, allowing the French King, Jean II, to move down to this region to confront Edward. He arrives unexpectedly with a huge army and anticipates a crushing victory against the smaller Anglo-Gascon force, which is short on supplies.

The battle: Edward has positioned his men, veterans led by experienced commanders, in such a way as to make maximum use of the broken ground and hedgerows. The French begin with a mad charge by a few hundred knights straight at the English positions, which only succeeds in leaving a pile of bodies and delivering the first of the day's prisoners. The remainder march forward on foot: wise advice in that it prevents the knights from losing their horses to arrow fire, though it wrecks their chances of getting into the fight untired and safe from repeated arrow volleys. The first line arrives and is enveloped. It breaks. It flees through the second, throwing it into disorder. The English get on their horses and pursue those fleeing, in the process slamming into the third row which was still advancing, and smashing it then in its flank to complete the French disaster. The French King, one of his sons, and a number of great nobles are captured. The Dauphin escapes, and is left to act as regent to a country caught in political turmoil.

Top tips: Even when the lines have broken, the French knights do fight on here and there. It's a matter of personal preference whether you take them on thinking these are probably the individuals with the highest ransom value, because they belong to important orders of chivalry forbidding them to run off, or instead opt to mount your horse and chase after some easier prey. The city of Poitiers closes its gates so you can capture prisoners right up to the walls; in the scramble to surrender some pursuers capture five or six. But avoid the jostle to capture the King of France as he'll aim for the knight with the best French accent.

(6) Otterburn 1388

The situation: The Scottish front provides a number of opportunities over the years for small scale raiding, and for being employed to push back the 'reivers'. It's important to remember though that it's not always plain sailing, certainly in terms of garrison work the further north you go. In the 1380s, the peace that followed Neville's Cross was still in place, but the Scots had failed to keep up with their ransom payments. In 1385, a force that included some French soldiers triggered some major border fighting. A large Scottish invasion followed in 1388. During one skirmish, the Scots captured the pennant from the lance of the son of the Earl of Northumberland, Henry "Hotspur" Percy, which may have encouraged him to give pursuit. He surprises the Earl of Douglas near the border.

The battle: The Scots are badly shaken by the unexpected arrival of a larger force and rush to make ready. Percy's forces are tired, but he decides to force battle. A force is sent to outflank the enemy and hit their camp in the rear. The English are initially successful but the right flank is then hit by a Scottish counterattack that Douglas has already prepped for. The English flanking attack misses the Scottish flankers, and hits the empty Scots camp in its turn. But the English are tired and unable to make best use of their missile strength. Douglas is killed, but Percy and his brother captured as the Scottish main force prevails.

Top tips: This is something of a night time slog. On arriving in the field, you'll have very little time so use it to grab a really quick snack from your bag as it may be your only chance. Mind the boggy ground, which will limit your mobility. Keep your wits about you, and an avenue open to retreat; don't get penned in with the main body. If you are going to get yourself captured, try to do it near Percy; thanks to his reputation for chivalry this day, his ransom is paid for by the King, and you might try to get some reflected glory and insurance cover by association.

(7) Pilleth 1402

The situation: Wales is in revolt. An attempt to suppress it merely delayed its spread. The Earl of March has been despatched to crush Glendower's forces, which lie just inside the Welsh border.

The battle: The engagement is fought on a steep slope, with Welsh archers holding the high ground just beyond a prominent and sturdy church. The advantage of height gives them crucial additional archery range, as Mortimer's troops soon find out. As the latter advance, hidden spearmen emerge from woods and thickets on their right flank. Welsh archers in Mortimer's ranks defect, and fire into his exposed men. Mortimer is captured; his army is destroyed; the dead go unburied.

Top tips: This is one battle you'd better avoid. The church does provide some cover, and is the scene of hard fighting, but it runs lengthwise down the slope and the field of protection is slim – only a couple of feet if you stick yourself behind the tower beside the main door. Don't hide inside it as it will catch fire. Round the side there's a pool which is reputed to have healing powers, especially for eyesight, though don't put too much faith in that today. Your escape route lies down the hill beyond arrowshot and away to the rear as you run. Don't loiter. The Welsh are now invading.

(8)   *Agincourt 1419*

The situation: Henry V has launched his expedition by landing in Normandy and taking Harfleur as a supply port. At the end of the campaigning season, he resolves to return by raiding through northern France. The French shadow the English, who begin to suffer from food shortages and an outbreak of dysentery. But while the English are steely in anticipating defeat, playing music and enjoying themselves on the eve of an expected trouncing, French morale is not helped by evil portents such as the bad luck sign of horses neighing in the night.

The battle: The French are numerically much stronger, some say by 6:1, though Henry's flanks are secured by the terrain. This funnels the French army across rough fields. Moreover, the French knights are all eager to be in the front line, leaving little room for arrow fodder and missile men to counteract the archers.

Unexpectedly, the English line advances to put the French under early missile range. Stakes are swiftly hammered in as field defences, and the arrows begin to drop. This triggers a charge by mounted French knights, who are driven back in confusion, straight through their own men now advancing on foot. It is a long walk through the mire that day, by a crowd of soldiers increasingly jostling for space in the narrow battlefield. The result is a press of French knights barely able to protect themselves as arrows rain down on them. Their mass pushes the first English line back, but soon they find themselves caught in a latter-day Cannae, squashed together, unable to defend themselves against the archers battering them with mallets or knifing them as they collapse in a quagmire of mud. The nobility of northern France is decimated.

Top tips: Henry V is up for some tough fighting today, so one route to personal advancement is to stick with him or the Duke of Gloucester and show some mettle as well as metal. Ignore the order to execute any prisoners you've taken, as the French won't attack again so you'll just lose a hostage. Don't leave any valuables in your tent as the baggage train will get pillaged. For what it's worth, the French leaders of the ransackers will get slung in prison for the massacre of prisoners they trigger, but that won't get you your fancy leggings back from the pilfering peasant.

(9)   Siege of Orleans 1428-9

The situation: The English and Burgundians are expanding their control of France. Orléans is a pivotal city; capturing it will ensure English control of the upper Loire, allowing a move on Angers downstream to link up English possessions north and south. The city sits beside a fortified bridge, crossing an island that makes for a good cannon emplacement for any siege. The defenders in advance have destroyed all outlying buildings including a dozen churches and priories.

The battle: The English quickly seize the key defences of the bridge. Unhappily, French reinforcements arrive, and the English Commander, Salisbury, is fatally wounded by a lucky cannon strike. That gives the defenders time to prepare. Most of the remainder is a story about a failed siege, where the attackers aren't strong enough to cut off the city completely. The English beat off an attack on their supply column (the Battle of the Herrings), which dents low French morale. But a supply train with Joan of Arc arrives to feed the city, and others follow. The English outworks are attacked in turn, not always with credible results on Joan's part, but the southern part of the siege works are eventually cleared and with it the siege is broken.

Top tips: With Joan in the neighbourhood, churches are again places of sanctuary. You can retreat into one of these to stop being automatically killed. Unfortunately, most were pulled down before you got here. We advise strategic discretion as the better part of valour.

(10)   Castillon 1453

The situation: After being ejected from France, the English are back to support a revolt in Gascony. They are heavily outnumbered, but when has that ever stopped them? Talbot advances to Castillon, one of the toll towns and part of the network of riverine towns providing waterborne links back to Bordeaux. An initial skirmish produces an early English victory, clearing the woods overlooking the town.

The battle: Talbot decides to engage the French when reports emerge of a French withdrawal. But in fact it's just the non-combatants who are being moved. The French outnumber the English, are in a fortified camp, are bordered by scraggy marsh, and have artillery set up. The result is a disaster. Talbot's men are already heavily engaged when Breton reinforcements now arrive in large number and hit him in the flank. He is killed and his army ruined. Many survive but are captured in town afterwards.

Top tips: Bordeaux will hold out yet for some time so the objective is to get back there. If you can, bolt back to Castillon, grab a small boat and head downstream along the Dordogne.

Stay away from the left flank. Don't loiter near Talbot unless you want to become a feature of the church that ends up built on his death place.

There's a long thin island off to the right but that won't keep you safe for too long, and the water is too fast flowing for many to cross without drowning. Aim for the ford which is a bit further upstream than your colleagues seem to think, then cross and hightail it back west. You are safe from pursuit once you pass St Émilion.

Battle cribsheet

The following is a list of the more important battles, so you know which ones to volunteer for, and when you need to claim you've come down with a mild dose of Black Death. We exclude sieges due to lack of space in a book

English victories are on white backgrounds, French ones are greyed.

Date of Battle	Name of the Battle	Result of the Battle (note the growth in French wins, shaded, as time goes on)
1337	**Battle of Cadsand**	**English victory.** Flemish defeated trying to evict pillagers. Minimal impact.
1339	**(First) Battle of Sluys**	**English victory.** Tends to get forgotten thanks to the 1340 battle. English pursue French shipping into the principle harbour of Flanders, but then get carried away and attack neutrals as well – for which hefty compensation will have to be paid.
1340	**Battle of Sluys**	**English victory.** Wreck of a major French fleet. A considerable propaganda coup.
1340	**Battle of St Omer**	**French victory.** Sally turns into a topsy turvy scrap, ending in an Anglo-Flemish rout abandoning most of their camp.

1342	Battle of Morlaix	**English victory.** French cavalry charge repulsed at cost.
1345	Battle of Auberoche	**English victory.** Initial French success reversed.
1346	Battle of Blanctaque	**English victory.** English force a passage across a marsh. French defeat allows English advance to continue.
1346	Battle of Crécy	**English victory.** Of huge strategic and tactical importance. North of France exposed.
1346	Battle of Saint-Pol-de-Leon	**English victory.** An outnumbered English force beats off French assaults and is able to withdraw in good order.
1346	Battle of Neville's Cross	**English victory.** Scots army pushed into attacking by archery, then defeated. David II captured. Neutralises the threat to Northern England for many years.
1347	Battle of La Roche-Derrien	**English victory.** Besiegers caught between a relief force and a sally. French defeated piecemeal. Their forces in Brittany savaged and need reorganising.
1347	Battle of Cassel	**Flemish victory.** French repulsed after hard fighting by timely deployment of heavy Flemish reserves.
1350	Battle of Winchelsea	**English victory.** Franco-Castilian fleet mauled.
1351	Battle of Saintes	**English victory.** French surprised in the field by a second English force arriving in their rear. Leaders captured, but local fort holds out.
1351	Battle of the Thirty	**Franco-Breton victory.** Anglo-Bretons lose combat of champions on a local issue.
1351	Battle of Ardres	**French victory.** Force from Calais is trapped by a river bend. French commander killed but English one captured.
1352	Battle of Mauron	**Anglo-Breton victory.** Heavy losses on both sides.
1354	Battle of Montmuran	**French victory.** Heavy English losses. Emergence of Bertrand du Guesclin.
1356	Battle of Poitiers	**English victory.** Tables turned by a badly exposed English expedition. Jean II captured. Central French government rule crumples.
1364	Battle of Cocherel	**French victory.** Du Guesclin defeats an undisciplined Anglo-Navarrese force. Paris safe.
1364	Battle of Auray	**English victory.** Du Guesclin captured, French claimant to Duchy of Brittany killed. Pro-English claimant wins but over the long term at the cost of feudal allegiance to France
1367	Battle of Najera	**English victory.** Enrique II soundly defeated. Pedro the Cruel restored to the throne of Castile. Du Guesclin again captured.

1369	Battle of Montiel	French victory. Pedro defeated then killed. French ally supreme in Castile. Naval balance tips towards French.
1370	Battle of Pontvallain	French victory. English forces are divided. In three engagements, Du Guesclin halts English advances in the north west, ends English reputation for victories, and confirms his authority as new Marshal.
1372	Battle of La Rochelle	Franco-Castilian victory. English fleet defeated, Earl of Pembroke captured, Poitou not reinforced.
1372	Battle of Soubise	French victory. Loss of Gascon field army and key commanders, including the heroic Captal de Buch, opens the door to France recapturing most of 'greater Gascony'.
1373	Battle of Chizé	French victory. After initial success, the English force is defeated and its captain taken. The rich territory of Poitou falls to the French.
1385	Battle of Aljubarrota	Portuguese-English victory. Attempts by Castilians to seize Portugal stopped. Portuguese independence secured. John of Gaunt drops his claim to the throne but marries off various children to Iberian monarchs. Castilian navy no longer a threat to England, and prospect of invasion of Gascony from the south ends.
1388	Battle of Otterburn	Marginal Scots victory. Rounds off a large Scottish raiding incursion. English surprise attack fended off. Henry "Hotspur" Percy captured, but important Earl Douglas killed.
1415	Battle of Agincourt	English victory. Huge defeat for the French with massive loss of life, including nobles. Exposed English forces saved. Considerable prestige loss by French, key nobles captive.
1416	Battle of Harfleur	English victory. French fleet defeated. English maintain lines of communication.
1421	Battle of Baugé (Loire)	Franco-Scots victory. Death of impetuous Duke of Clarence, Henry's brother and at that point the heir presumptive.
1423	Battle of Cravant	Anglo-Burgundian victory. First allied victory, heavy Scots casualties.
1424	Battle of Verneuil	Anglo-Burgundian victory. Larger French forces again smashed. Archers remarkably survive being charged through by the first wave which continues on to the baggage. Remainder of the French forces then pummelled. Further massive Scots casualties. English conquests in North West France secured.
1427	Battle of Montargis	French victory. English attempt to storm the town, but floods cut off half their force, which is defeated: the other half routs.
1427	Battle of Ambrières	French victory. Sir John Falstoff defeated in a small battle, which triggers a revolt in Maine against English rule.
1429	Battle of the Herrings (Rouvray)	English victory. Falstoff fights off an attack. His supply column reaches the besiegers at Orleans. Terrible impact on French defenders only salvaged by Joan of Arc's arrival. The city is on the cusp of surrendering.

1428 - 1429	Siege of Orleans	**French victory** from several battles around the site of the siege. Securing Orléans saves French positions in the Loire and rallies morale.
1429	Battle of Patay	**French victory.** Post-Orleans French offensive. Disorganised English lines, whose positions are betrayed by responses to a stag running through them. Talbot is defeated. French can now concentrate on the north. French king can now be crowned in Rheims, legitimising his cause.
1435	Battle of Gerbevoy	**French victory.** Death of Earl of Arundel from wounds, thus loss of important veteran general.
1436	Battle of Epincy	**Franco-Burgundian victory.** The small English field army is removed. Paris exposed to French conquest.
1437	Battle of Ry	**English victory.** French move on Rouen fails, and is then defeated by Talbot. Tenuous English hold on Normandy saved.
1450	Battle of Formigny	**Franco-Breton victory.** English field army removed. Normandy exposed to French conquest.
1453	Battle of Castillon	**French victory.** Death of Talbot and his eldest son. Guarantees the final loss of Bordeaux, and end of the Wars.

Chapter 5
Meet and greet

Why focus on culture and sites when you have the opportunity to meet some fascinating, unique, and sometimes utterly crazy people? Here's our guide to a tiny selection of some of the leading characters of this age for pressing the flesh. Ideally without armaments involved.

High Season 1337 - 1369

The key figure behind the Hundred Years War, whatever your political viewpoint, has to be **Edward III of England** (r.1327-1377).

Edward III: All down to him.

Notwithstanding the provocations, he properly-speaking starts it; and his decisions early on mean that it can only end with a radical power shift. You'll probably enjoy meeting him: people do tend to flock to his side. He's quite well read for the age, a fine horseman and knight. His early years mark him out in particular. He starts in life in exile with his mother, giving him some polish of travel. But the deposition and murder of his father in a plot involving his mother leads to him managing a youthful coup of his own. An unhappy upbringing has lent him the air of a plotter, a degree of impulsiveness, and a penchant for calculated risks, particularly when exploiting the problems of others. He can be short-termist and likes to get the advice he expects to hear. His chivalry is tarnished; he's prepared to offer to fight a duel, but also when it doesn't suit him to duck one; he's also ready to execute prisoners if basic codes and expectations are broken.

We offer a couple of basic tips for you. His lodgings burned down at the start of the conflict in Flanders almost killing him, so don't leave candles burning overnight as this might annoy him. Also, don't ask about his family. His mother is imprisoned by him in Castle Rising in Norfolk. Edward's last years mark a precipitous decline, an over-reliance on unpopular councillors, and senility, which helps to explain how the French manage to salvage their situation.

Edward's leading protagonist, at least at the outset, is his French counterpart **Philip VI** (1293-1350). He's also known as the Fortunate, which properly speaking only applies to his initial circumstances because he wasn't expecting to become king, and some unkindly say it shows. He's personally brave but a cautious general, when not being a disastrous one by being pushed into attacks on well-defended positions. He's moody, indecisive, superstitious, and picks a bad choice of adviser (mostly lawyers and bishops, which bodes ill for a war). He can kill for political advantage, and is terrified of treason. He's also increasingly fat, which might be what encourages Edward III to tempt him into trying to squeeze into some armour. As the wars progress his is unhappier company. But what a glittering star is the French court at the start. Perhaps it's encapsulated in a single locket you might catch sight of, the small golden treasure Philip keeps with its hidden compartments showing beautiful lacquered portraits and holding a relic from the crown of thorns.

As we are in the company of kings, let's turn to **David II of Scotland** (1324-1371). You've sadly timed your arrival poorly, because you've just lucked out on meeting the remarkable Robert the Bruce. Still, you can get one generation away and meet his son. He's spent a lot of his youth in exile in France. Thanks to the Battle of Neville's Cross, you can drop by to see him in London. Something of a bon viveur, he can be personally bold but also pragmatic in the face of reduced circumstances.

Far be it for us merely to point you in the direction of eminent monarchs. The great **Petrarch** is out of reach over in Italy, but there's his contemporary **William of Ockham** (1287-1347). He is one of the West's great thinkers of the time. Unfortunately, right now he's over in Germany but you can still discuss his thinkings with a number of his old associates. Ockham's infamous for having been tasked to investigate Franciscan vows of poverty, and finding his boss's position (which unsurprisingly rather appreciated a wealthy church) heretical. Correspondingly he's a controversial character. He's also a widely published philosopher. The most celebrated idea associated with him, Ockham's Razor, properly speaking isn't his idea at all: basically, it holds that explanations usually turn out to be the simplest. Ockham himself only says the explanation can be self-evident, known from experience, or mentioned in scripture – we might cite the example that a flood may be coming if it rains a lot, it flooded this time last year, or we have seen a lot of sinning going on. But the mere fact his name has been associated with the idea says something about his broader popularity (notwithstanding his excommunication on the Franciscan thing).

Jean II (or John II) of France (1319-1364) is another royal captive you can get to meet in person. He gets a lot of bad press as a result. He's quite capable of wandering into legal grey areas, including executing hostages that displease him. He's aggressive, can 'forget' debts to people he doesn't like, and quite willing to foist unpopular taxes on the public. But he's also a remarkable man of honour, returning to English captivity when his captured son does a runner.

John II: Doing time.

His opponent on the battlefield is the exemplar of knightly worth. **Edward, the Black Prince** is a veteran of both Crécy and Poitiers along with numerous scraps and sieges. Never forget where he gets his name from, the massacre of the townsfolk of Limoges who resisted

Black by name, black by nature

longer than was prudent. To be fair, they had defected to the French, contrary to a recent treaty; its bishop had been godfather to one of his sons; he had made a serious oath of revenge on hearing the news he had to uphold; and the territory was properly speaking not even French in the first place but part of the Breton patrimony. So perhaps we can excuse him a little, even if his contemporaries don't. His man management skills away from the battlefield also leave a lot to be desired. We council not asking after his health (atrocious in his last year, possibly dropsy) or his family (his elder son, Edward, dies when just a child).

There are a number of remarkable military figures over this period. **Thomas de Beauchamp, 11th Earl of Warwick** (1313-1369) provides as good an example as any. He's one of the original Garter knights, fights as a senior commander at Calais, Scotland, Crécy and Poitiers, and even campaigns on a crusade with the Teutonic Knights in eastern Europe. This makes him an excellent person to chat to about travel advice, particularly in areas requiring hard hats. His wife is also an interesting character as a Mortimer.

You may never have heard of **Philippe de Vitry** (1291-1361) but that's an omission you can correct. He's an ambassador and bishop, but also as it happens one of the century's leading scholars and composers. He's a major supporter of new methods in annotating music, and designing and developing motets, typically in Latin and generally quite complex. At least keep an ear open for his works during your visits to abbeys and churches. Petrarch likes them.

If you want to meet the remarkable adventurer **Sir John Hawkwoode** (1320-1394), this is the time to do it. Hawkwoode is stuck in France after the battle of Poitiers stops play. Rather than return home, he decides to take his military skills a little further away than most. He heads to Italy, and

Paliano Italiano?

assumes control of the mercenary band known as the White Company. For the next thirty years he is involved in the great wars of the northern city states, employed by most of them at one stage or another. A respected friend of Milan, he dies on the eve of his retirement in England as the general of Florence. Not bad for the son of a tanner.

Of slightly less plebeian birth, but equally venerated in his home country, is **Jacob van Artevelde** (1295-1345). Van Artevelde is of the Flemish gentry, emerging as one of the figures of urban independence. As the wool embargo bites into the economy of the area, he leads his townspeople into increasingly siding with the English, other key towns then following suit. He assumes a paramount position in Ghent and is inspirational in bringing the towns of Flanders into a working alliance. He's competent and savvy. However, his pre-eminence and support for closer English rule prove his undoing, and he is killed by a mob – always a danger in popular insurrections. He's a fascinating person to meet as a counterpoint to Philip VI as a lesson in how people react to power creeping or rushing over them. Jacob's son Philip will be a chip off the old block too.

On the theme of the hoy polloy, we mustn't overlook farmer **Guillaume Cale** (d.1358). You might hear him talked about as 'Jacques Bonhomme', and being called Joe Bloggs helps in an age where identity is a dangerous piece of information to be waving about. He's the leader of the 'Jacques', France's earlier and rather more brutal version of the Peasants' Revolt. Van

Artevelde's reputation grew because he was fighting for his people as well as for his social class; Cale's misfortune is that he's French and thus a plain rebel. After the disaster of Poitiers, the French monarchy loses its grip on much of its territory. Around Beauvais, a brutal insurgency flashes amongst the poorest, that kills, burns and rapes those with money and status. There are reports of the vilest excesses, such as roasting a knight and then trying to force his family to eat him. Copycat actions make the terrors spread like wildfire. Cale's reputation puts him at the forefront of the atrocities: this may be unfair as it seems he seeks to avoid becoming leader. But his intelligence and speaking skills (plus good looks) makes him the obvious candidate for chief head in the noose. He enters into contact with **Etienne Marcel** and the social revolutionaries in Paris seeking government more to the liking of the merchants and urban workers. The link up is brief; Cale's control over the many roving bands is minimal; and his opponent uses treachery. Invited to a parley, he's instead seized, tortured and executed. His demoralised army is attacked and obliterated, and the whole region is utterly devastated as a punishment.

On a positive note, his treacherous murderer **Charles, King of Navarre** (1332-1387) has a bad end. Charles is ambitious, untrustworthy, scheming and not above using poison. A major early player with a claim on the French throne in his own right (and properly speaking, better than the English one), his aspirations to grab huge chunks of inheritance in Normandy and northern France never quite work out. Charles will end his days recovering from loose living by being wrapped in a huge bandage soaked in brandy. A servant then unwisely tries to singe some loose threads with a candle. Clearly the health and safety aspects of linen and naked flames are not picked up on by contemporaries (see later).

Mid Season 1369- 1415

Charles V of France (1338-1380) earns the sobriquet 'the Wise'. It's during the Mid Season that you can see this the clearest. The 1350s after the Battle of Poitiers are rough times, with the prince getting involved in political assassinations after two of his own councillors are murdered. His generals also get mauled in Brittany. But from 1369 the tide of war turns and all of England's gains end up nullified. Charles is another bon viveur, a thinker and man of faith, but who is driven to involve himself in the Avignon dispute and in the process exacerbating it. He has a very tough start, from which he learns. Clever, bold, but physically weak, he is a patron of the arts.

Charles's good fortune is to have a solid general. **Bertrand du Guesclin** (1320-1380) is short, stout as a barrel, and a frightening powerhouse of armoured wrath on the battlefield. He leads and inspires by example rather than excessive competence, his steady methodological approach meaning French advantages are not thrown away rashly. Constable of France under Charles V, he busies himself gradually rolling back the English lines. Du Guesclin is ruthless, cruel, indiscriminate, has long arms and has a face like a toad. But we wouldn't tell him any of that. He has a habit of being single minded in his vengeance.

What a contrast to the next generation on the English side. **Henry 'Hotspur' Percy** (1364-1403) is handsome, dashing, honourable, gallant, marginally incompetent, and ultimately a traitor. As a Percy, his card is marked from the outset as the dividing lines are drawn up between the claimants after Richard II is deposed. But that won't detract from a reputation already gained against the Scots at Otterburn and later Homildon Hill. Hotspur and Prince Harry meet in battle outside Shrewsbury; both are hit in the face by arrows. The Prince is the lucky one that day.

Geoffrey Chaucer (1343-1400) is the £16 man. That at least was his ransom from the French when he was captured fighting for Edward III, so we know his value before he became a celebrated author. It's perhaps best for his bank balance that he wasn't captured later. His background is as a trusted servant of some standing, indeed on occasion a diplomat, a position made more fortunate by being related to a wife of the royal duke John of Gaunt though these also will associate him with lean political times. His most celebrated work is his Canterbury Tales, but his poems are also well received. Chaucer's an innovative writer, well-versed and lively. Most important of all, like his colleague **William Langland** the author of the dream sequence known as Piers Ploughman, he's exploring the medium of literary English rather than French, and with it developing a distinct national identity. Chaucer's well-read, well-connected, and married to a Gascon. He's also not the best manager, and not above getting involved in scurvy dealings. But at the end of his life he's ensconced in a house just beside the top end of Westminster Abbey so drop by on him if you are passing through.

A very different man of the people is **Wat Tyler** (d. 1381). A Maidstone man, he emerges as the leader of the Kent rebels during the time of the Peasants' Revolt. Before you leap to ready conclusions, consider just why all those stories about Robin Hood start becoming very popular in the 1370s. It's because the country is feeling the weight of taxes, people think they're unfair, and everyone is urging on an underdog hero. Come the Revolt everyone's a Little John or Will Scarlet. Rather than taxing wealth, the king is now taxing heads – a poll tax, and by 1381 it's in its fourth year in a row rather than being a rare and exceptional event. The Revolt needs leaders. Tyler's a self-confident man, a knife-wielding ruffian who's quick to anger, who certainly doesn't keep within life's station judging by how he manhandles a king and then gargles in his august presence. On the plus side, he likes his beer (he is from Kent). We wouldn't get too close to him, or be caught laughing at his tiny horse.

For contrast, go and visit the celebrated **Dick Whittington** (d.1423). Sir Richard is not as it turns out a peasant who's made good. His family are well off and he's made money in the wool trade before becoming Lord

Ringing in your ears? Go back to work then.

Mayor of London, a post he'll hold no fewer than four times. So don't disappoint yourself from the outset thinking you'll hear a rags-to-riches story, or expect anything about him having been about to quit because he keeps getting beaten up as an apprentice, and is en route out of the city when he hears bells chiming that seem to tell him to turn round. But he is a generous donor to good causes, and the word is that his will is packed with donations setting up charitable foundations that will help a lot of people in the capital for many a long year to come. We've never actually seen him with a cat; maybe that would make a good present for him if you're visiting.

Few people don't have an opinion about **John Wycliffe** (1324-1384). An Oxford man of Yorkshire upbringing, he is borrowed by the King to accompany a mission to the Pope. This draws him into the orbit of John of Gaunt (Henry IV's father), a useful protector in the troubled debates over church reform triggered by the Lollards. Wycliffe's a great opponent of church wealth, in a sense merely following on in Ockham's tracks. From those great questions about church finances, he comes to challenge its authority, and then its sacraments. He's clever (with John Purvey, he translates the Bible into English for the first time), a little scrawny, and a rough critic.

Another person who gets bad press is **Richard II** (1367-1400). His handling of the Peasants Revolt while still only fourteen shows early aplumb. He's cultured, but arbitrary and authoritarian to the point of

Richard II: A man of opportunity and risk.

brutality, and relies heavily (like his late father) on unpopular advisers combined with an absolutist approach. He sustains peace with France (on diminished frontiers) but has a bad war in Ireland. Ultimately, he pushes his close family - and competing heirs - too far and there's a coup. Murdering and exiling the nearest of them might have contributed; he has a habit of escalating punishments beyond what's reasonable. Stick on the right side of this petty dictator and you'll be richly rewarded, but get out while the going's good and before advisers start getting knifed.

Richard's successor is Henry Bolingbroke who becomes **Henry IV** (1367-1413). Please him, and he might honour you with one of his gifts of fine enamel jewellery he so likes. He's the first king since the Conquest whose first language is English. Away from the social circuit, Henry's main task is defensive, keeping hold of power once seized, suppressing rebellions especially Glendower's, and pushing back Scottish and French incursions. Executing the Archbishop of York for treason is technically correct and well-founded, but makes people nervous about annoying God. So too does marrying Joan of Navarre. This is a sound political alliance as remarriages go, but people think she's a witch. No wonder people are saying that the King's illness is leprosy mixed in with epilepsy brought on by divine retribution. On top of all that, Henry IV prefers French peace, but Prince Henry prefers to exploit French weakness and invade. It does nothing for family relations. Someone should write a play about it.

Welsh bowmen and spearmen make up a significant part of the armies of the English monarchs. But there's also a season where they are fighting for themselves. Under the leadership of **Owain Glyndwyr** (Owen Glendower, Owen ap Glendourdy, 1354-1415), the Welsh for one last time find a prince from their own ruling dynasties. He's a Powys man, a landowner in north Wales, who has studied law in London and served with the Bolingbrokes. But on his return home he becomes involved in a dispute with a neighbour. With false charges of treason being floated, the argument escalates into full blown rebellion. His successes lead to the capture of most of Wales and recognition by France, but the defeat of his allies in England means the tide is turning and a future as a rebel in the hills will be his end. With an independent Greater Wales in sight but never attained, Glendower's successes prove as promising but as hollow as Henry V's. But if you're in Wales to chase him, seek out instead **Dafydd Gam**. This character is Glendower's bitter enemy, a Brecon loyalist with a dodgy eye, who captures Glendower's son, tries to assassinate the father at the new Welsh Parliament, and then betrays an oath when set free. On the plus side, he'll redeem himself by sterling if fatal service at Agincourt.

Low Season 1415 - 1453

Although he's barely round long enough to enjoy it, the key character of this period has to be

Henry V (1386-1422). His principal contribution is to pile into the French civil war with such military success the Gallic crown is knocked off its feet for two decades. In other circumstances and had he lived, his descendants might become Kings of a united England and France, but notwithstanding the legal niceties of a treaty that lawfully gives it to them others also have something to say on the matter. He's a valiant and brave knight, who gained much of his experience from fighting in Wales, and equally harsh on anyone who disobeys an order. Yet he's also interested in music (being a musician himself) and well educated. He's a good administrator and reformer, contrasting favourably with that other knightly hero his

Tragic haircut, tragic end.

great uncle the Black Prince. He begins to unify the whole of the country by establishing English as the language of government and society. On the other hand, he really does not get on well with his father – he possibly even got on better with the man his father deposed - and there is endless talk of double dealing or even plotting. Best to keep the family out of any conversation; it doesn't end well for any of them. His death is by dysentery which is not a happy way to go.

Some say Henry made a change when he became King, losing his previous penchant for fine wines, fast horses and loose living. This is unfair on **Sir John Falstolfe** (1378-1459), master of the Duke of Bedford's household, whom we have never seen drinking madly but did once see fighting valiantly at a battle to stop some rather plain fishy foodstuffs getting into the English camp during the siege of Orleans. We suspect he'd only go into a tavern because there was an opportunity to buy it at a discount.

Henry's opponent, and the father of his future bride, is the unfortunate **Charles VI of France** (1368-1422). A lavish joker, he loves jousting, but is not a natural leader. Worse, his reign consists of bouts of insanity mingled with periods of normality, sometimes snapping swiftly between the two. When he's himself, Charles is kind, thoughtful, tall and energetic. But after an illness in which his hair falls out, he makes the mistake of ignoring medical advice and setting out on a military expedition during a baking hot day. First he bumps into a wild character who accosts the party with words about betrayal. Then clearly the heat, reflected off the scorched sand and exacerbated by his black velvet costume, and the bright light reflected off the glinting armour gets to him. A butterfingers squire makes a clatter with a lance, and Charles flips. He chases his terrified brother around and savagely attacks several of his party before dropping comatose. He does recover but it's not the only unhappy incident. The following year, the king hosts a party in which he and four friends wrap themselves up in linen as fancy dress and jump around as wild men. They sadly forget the safety precautions and go up in flames when they get too near a torch: Charles narrowly escapes thanks to a quick-thinking duchess with voluminous flame-retardant skirts. This naturally triggers another mental episode. If you go to see him during one of these bad turns, be mindful that he may not recognise his own name or rank; bring something for the princes as they may be badly looked after; and approach him with caution, as he may be armed and psychotic, badly unwashed and very smelly, or thinking he's made of glass and liable to break. It's wise not to be judgmental: everyone else in Christendom already is, calling it divine retribution and blaming it one way or another on French politics involving the Great Schism at Avignon.

Charles's heir one day will become **Charles VII of France** (1403-1461), but for now he's just the Dauphin, the ruler of the Dauphiné, a region of southern France. He's the eleventh child of the royal family, which says something about how unwell his elder brothers are. He's also later disowned by his mother as the illegitimate offspring of an affair with the king's brother during the royal madness. That turns out to be one affair amongst many. Definitely do not mention her in his presence. Don't pontificate: he is said to be terrified of bridges as the result of witnessing a murder up close on one. After a flaky start, he grows in stature with success. He's not afraid to take on the Church, his Pragmatic Sanction of Bourges in 1438 in particular laying down markers on what the Pope could do in French territory. He also starts to close the lid on the independent power of his nobles. He's a strong patron of the arts, enjoys luxury, and – another innovation – openly has powerful mistresses, which is something of a shift from his very devout youth, especially as he treats them better than he does his wife. His interest is in unifying the country, so he's prepared to be generous in victory. He's additionally a prompt and fair payer of debts, and prepared to take a more peaceful and less risky route to success even if less glory is attached.

Some of his success can be attributed to **Joan of Arc** (1411-1431). We suggest dropping by and visiting her at Domremy over in the east of France, before the fame builds up. Don't call her a shepherdess as she only does that now and again to help out with the family smallholding: her family is well-to-do and they live in a jaunty two storey affair by the bank of a stream, with a fine view overlooking pleasant water meadows. She's also been a chambermaid in an inn, and done boyish tasks such as looking after the horses. Then she hears voices telling her to get the Dauphin crowned. This doesn't endear her to everybody, especially those who personally stand to lose from risky military adventures or think she's a crank. But she's certainly got a sense of her own significance, plus she somehow knows a personal secret of the Dauphin so she wins him round. It doesn't make her arrow proof and her luck is finite. She's wounded at Orleans. She's wounded again and defeated before Paris. She then heads off to Normandy, without success, and then Compiegne where she's captured by the Burgundians.

The King of France does nothing, despite having an important prisoner of his own he could swap. She's sold on, and the University of Paris resolves she should be tried by the Inquisition. A French court finds her guilty of blasphemy, schism, of believing herself in personal communion with saints, cross-dressing against divine law, sedition, rejecting the Pope, inhumane cruelties and impersonating a knight. She recants, but then is found in her cell in men's clothes once again. She's burned at the stake.

Flame retardant gloves are not universal.

All in all, it's a high flying life as far as Orleans and then downhill all the way from there, betrayed by those she had gone to help and who clearly saw her as a discardable tool. Does she deserve her fame? What's certain is that before she turns up, the French feel as if they are in a losing rut. In a feudal society dependent on local support, morale and reputation is vitally important in winning the war of loyalties. She might not be the sharpest axe amongst the military planners, but she does restore the military initiative to the French and give Charles VII the preconditions to become a legitimate alternative claimant to running France. She's also quite capable of executing a tough fighter when he's taken prisoner to make a point. Her reputation improves with time when in the end she's proved right on who was going to win; for now views on her are very mixed, and extreme.

Another controversial character in the French arsenal, and one you want to steer well clear of, is **Gilles de Rais** (1404-1440). Despite being a close associate of Joan, this fellow is certainly not touched by any heavenly voices. A Breton, he rises to the rank of Constable of France. He subsequently retires back to his estates. But despite immense wealth, his luxurious lifestyle means he is dissipating his wealth, and he turns from being a patron of the arts in desperation into becoming a patron of an alchemist and demonologist. De Rais is arrested by his enemy the Duke of Brittany and charged with horrendous sex crimes and murders of dozens of children. Needless to say, he is executed.

Compared with this dreaded man, the foibles of the English leaders seem tiny. The main fault of **Henry VI** (1421-1471), other than being a mere baby when his father dies, is his utterly unsuited character. At least Joan of Arc could stab you with a sword. Henry doesn't really want to be king. He's gentle, and kindly, and uncertain, and vacillating, and only as good as the last adviser who speaks to him. He's loyal and honourable, but assumes everyone else to be so too. In another life he would have been a happy scholar at one of the colleges he founded. He is a fine person to dine with, but cross your fingers in a crisis, of which there are increasingly many.

Henry's fortunate in at least having some good military commanders working for him, and in his early years has a capable uncle working as his French regent. **John, Duke of Bedford** (1389-1435) is synonymous with the high water mark for England. He marries the sister of the Duke of Burgundy, creating a vital personal link, for as long as she lives. A fair and capable manager and diplomat, he is also key in founding the University of Caen, which later briefly flourishes as a counter to that of Paris once it's back in French hands. But contrast him with **Humphrey, Duke of Gloucester** (1391-1447). The plaudits this royal brother gains from work at Agincourt are surpassed by later failures. He foolishly annoys the Burgundians by trying to marry into one of their senior families, and manages to ruin any chances of peace on favourable terms by pushing for war into a period where England can no longer win it. If he dabbles in the occult it's astrology rather than anything Gilles de Rais would try to summon in a pentagram; but his mistress manages to get herself accused of witchcraft by her frivolities. He may be popular on the street, but his judgment leaves much to be desired.

Henry is better served by the likes of **John Talbot** (1387-1453). While the number of interesting commanders out in the field means we can't dwell on them all, Talbot stands out for several reasons. A quarrelsome type in peace, he is amongst the kingdom's foremost captains in war. His efforts in keeping hold of Normandy despite the tide deservedly lead him to be made Earl of Shrewsbury. His life is not without reverses: he's captured fighting against Joan of Arc's forces, and later again after the loss of Rouen; part of the deal for his later freedom is that he'll avoid wearing full armour when fighting the French (which makes life on the front line somewhat hazardous). The fact that he fights on, and commands the forlorn final battle, makes him in the eyes of many the Last Knight, and the epitome of the end of the age of chivalry.

On which subject, we close our tour of the great and not-so-good with two rascals. **Jack Cade** (d.1450) some say is of Irish origin and a murderer to boot, but then he gets a lot of bad press or maybe people are mixing him up with someone else in the crowd. He's the fellow who emerges from the Kentish mass that descends on London for redress against a number of government faults, mainly about bad government, trade difficulties, self-serving royal advisers, and bribery in the law courts. Cade tries, and generally fails, to stop the excesses of the mob. The atrocities indeed do turn London against them. The agents of the Crown hand out pardons, and Cade himself gets one; unfortunately, as he's been going around by the name of John Mortimer, his is issued in that name so technically he's not protected. Cade's not stupid and knows the trouble he's in, but is caught before he can escape and is fatally wounded.

The background of **Francois Villon** (b. 1431) is more genuinely thuggish. He's from a poor family, and after the death of his father is looked after by a local priest. It doesn't seem to have rubbed off, but right now Villon's studying at the Sorbonne and looking promising, so it's a good moment to visit this future great figure of literature. Come a couple of years after the Low Season ends, however, and he's killed someone in a brawl and committed a robbery. He spends many of the following years dodging lengthy spells in prison by good fortune and escaping execution by the skin of his teeth. But for his faults he is a great poet, sometimes acerbic, sometimes moving, and when pleading for the passer-by not to mock his gibbet has clearly been inspired by his own presence on death row. Truly as this age closes, where now indeed are the snows of yesteryear?

Chapter 7
Where to Visit

With an abundance of picturesque towns, seemly villages and impressive monuments, it's difficult to draw up an itinerary that can take in more than just a handful of the must-see sites. But whether you are passing through in prayer or in plunder, here's a suggestion of some of the key locations you'd miss having missed.

London and its surroundings

The capital of the English empire, such as an itinerant court allows, London is fast growing in importance as the fourteenth century advances. Its fortunes wax as its rival, Paris, wanes. Only two fifths of the size of the latter at the start of the Hundred Years War, and certainly eclipsed by the latter's splendour, London is spared the horrors of war and occupation if not the terrors and decimation of the Plague.

The key thing to remember about the place is that it's a tale of two cities. The London you are probably looking for is **the City of London**, which lies lower down the Thames to the east. This is the site of the old Roman city, though precious little evidence remains of it now except for some sequestered walls. The site is important. If Westminster is the lowest point a man can cross the river on foot, albeit getting wet, the City is the highest point upriver a sea-going boat can follow the tide and properly dock. That makes it the merchants' destination, and the home to a great collection of guilds and the home to the main Hanse community in the country. An old stone bridge from King John's time straddles the river, and as you'd expect it's littered with houses and even the customary chapel, this one to St Thomas Beckett. In troubled times, you might spot a celebrity or two looking down on you. This is where the heads of traitors are impaled after their death as a warning to others.

Navigating around town is quite easy. The Thames delineates the entire south of the city; beside this by the Strand sits the **Palace of Savoy**, the residence of the Duke of Lancaster (until Wat Tyler's men burn it down). The main thoroughfare is Cheapside. The river Fleet delineates the edge of the built up area to the west, short of the main city walls. The Walbrook divides the city in two as in Roman times, running down the centre and bisecting. The Houndsditch runs east-west short of the boundaries; we wouldn't recommend glancing into it if you walk past. But the most obvious reference point lies to the south east - the impressive keep of **the Tower of London**. Edward I built it up into an impressive fortress, which proved handy for Edward II who found it a safer residence than others. In Edward III's time though you'll definitely have to visit, as this is where the captured nobility and royalty of France are held. Their conditions as prisoners are good, as befitting their rank, and visitors of the appropriate status are welcomed. Not, though, ones of inappropriate status, though some of Wat Tyler's folk manage to barge their way in. Let's hope for your sake you aren't brought in via the waterfront through Traitor's Gate: your stay is not likely to end well.

London's not a university town, or the seat of an archbishop. But it does have the abbey of Greyfriars, which is a reputed centre of younger schooling. Of its religious buildings, St Paul's cathedral is a mighty structure, one of the longest and tallest buildings in Europe with its lofty spire and stretched-out transepts that make the surrounding houses look like minnows in the company of a whale. In the churchyard is a cross where open air preachers gather, and it's worth dropping by to see if someone of note is in town to lambast church failings in the Lollard debates. Another pastime is to head off to the elms of Tyburn, which is acquiring a reputation as the go-to place to watch public executions of criminals.

Notwithstanding the palaces of nobles in the town, bear in mind the city is still very much under development. Hold your nose and tread warily. Out in more open spaces, watch out for a favourite London pastime, quantains. Londoners have a reputation for being quite good horsemen, and this sport involves jousting at wooden figures while avoiding being struck by the spun image as you pass.

By contrast, the **City of Westminster** (reachable by road or by ferry) is the heart of government. It lies on the Thames opposite Lambeth Palace, where for the last hundred years the Archbishop of Canterbury has his London home, within walking distance of the Black Prince's mansion. Centrally located in this complex is the great Abbey. This holds the shrine of its founder, St Edward the Confessor, and has been the site of every coronation since the Conquest. It's in the same Gothic style you see in other great religious buildings of the last century. It's only been reconsecrated within a lifetime, and only recently that the country's dead kings have begun to be laid to rest there on their passing. You swiftly observe the magnificence that this royal patronage has brought.

The Abbey is also associated with Parliament. Initially, the Commons sits on its own in the Chapter House of the Abbey, a fine and bright room where everyone can see each other, but hardly custom made. Fifty years later they are based in the Refectory; we are not sure if this is an allegorical move, or to do with being closer to the catering.

The Abbey and its fine gardens and orchards sits the royal domain. **The Palace of Westminster** opposite is the estate of the monarch, and lies on an island part-enclosed within a belt of marsh. This is where Parliament often used to sit before the Commons split. The Lords still occasionally assemble here, but avoid that site (notable only for some tapestries) and aim for the Painted Chamber. It's a small room but has some striking historical murals, said to be the oldest set of genuinely English paintings around. It also has the King sleeping in it if you time it badly.

Don't think of chancing your luck with a dash to the Jewel Tower: that is the treasury, where the jewels and silver plate are kept. On the other hand, the great Norman chamber of William Rufus, **Westminster Hall**, once the largest European public space outside of Constantinople, is more accessible. It is the home of the great courts of Chancery, and of the Treasury – the alternative name of the latter, the Exchequer, comes from the lined table cloth you can see spread out. Great coronation events are also held here, under the magnificent hammer-beamed roof that Edward III has begun to construct. If you are attending one, bring waterproof leggings. It has been known to flood.

To the west of the cities, a useful way station lies at Windsor. This is an imposing old castle which Edward III is spending a lot of energy, and money, on rendering even more impressive. In the 1360s, he sets about creating the beautiful St George's Hall as the geographic centrepiece for his new Order of the Garter.

Southern England

London is a gateway city thanks to its sea links. Yet with the variable sailing conditions you are more likely to arrive in England at a harbour out in the provinces. Foremost amongst these used to be the **Cinque Ports**, a collection of harbours in the south east of the country facing the continent. As the name suggests, this is an association of five coastal towns, whose strategic importance led to kings giving them both rights and duties in order to best defend themselves and their area from sudden threat and invasion.

The original ports were **Hastings, Romney, Hythe, Dover and Sandwich.** A number of other coastal communities, called limbs, over time were co-opted to assist in supplying ships to meet the set naval obligations, in return for which they were granted some of the privileges too. As the towns changed in relative importance, full membership rights were correspondingly modified. Hastings has been in decline thanks to its beach drifting. An unwalled fishing town with a doddery castle, being sacked by the French does not help: its leading export in 1339 is the corpses the French grotesquely take back with them as trophies. Dover continues to retain its ancient importance thanks to a bay dominated by a serious castle. New Romney gained full Cinque Port status, but then a storm shifted the route of the river that gave its ships access, so now is back to being a marshland village with an unexpected bold and almost Flemish-looking church. Rye is walled – useful for trying to work out which port is going to be sacked next by the French. Winchelsea is a major and walled settlement but looking at ruin thanks to silting and a coming French raid. Ramsgate is not much more than a hamlet. Faversham has a royal abbey and the advantage of a Thames link to London. Margate is up and coming with a new harbour, its first. Lydd's church is visible for miles across the marshes. Tenterden is a very late addition to the list, thanks to its developing tradition of ship building. Wherever you pick though, you'll find places of character. Avoid the French tourists, though. They bring trouble.

Inland from the Kent coast, you'll need to plan somewhere to stay on your road to the capital. We recommend Thurnham Castle.

Artist: Casper Johnson (c) Kent County Council

The castle itself has been here for some time, perhaps from as far back as the Conquest. It overlooks the more recent village of the same name which has emerged as one of several villages that follow the base of the North Downs along a line of freshwater springs, always a bonus for travellers.

There's a hundred year old church and a manor. But take this opportunity to visit the castle as it will be abandoned by the fifteenth century when the owners move to a hall nearby.

Late visitors may care to note that enough remains of the site to make a modern visit worthwhile. In 1999 Kent County Council, with support from the Heritage Lottery Fund, English Heritage, RLCI, Maidstone Borough Council and Thurnham Parish Council, acquired the castle in order to conserve it and make it accessible.

Thurnham is one of three medieval earthwork castles in this part of the North Downs. The others are Binbury Castle (on the Detling Aerodrome Estate) and Stockbury Castle.

Those interested in learning more about medieval life in Kent can visit one of the county's many museums, helpfully listed in the recreational section of the county council website: http://www.kent.gov.uk

---

The head town of Kent however is **Canterbury.** It's long centuries now since it was the capital city of a tiny kingdom, but it's the head city of a province. That's because the place is the site of the headquarters of the Catholic Church in England, and the home of the leading Archbishop. If there's only one sight you see in town, it has to be the cathedral. It's a draw for pilgrims for long leagues thanks to the tomb of St Thomas, who's worked many a miracle here so if you have any conditions or ailments a detour is worth your time. Properly speaking, the place is a monastery so you may be lucky and find you can overnight on site, if you can put up with the noisy work being done on the Lanfranc Nave and the installation of the cloister vaulting. Otherwise, ask for a space at the Eastbridge Hospital. Avoid St Nicholas' as that is for lepers.

Beyond the abbey precincts, the castle won't distract you for long. Try the marketplace as the city is noted for its leather products, and don't forget of course to buy a pilgrimage trinket.

One castle with royal links is a definite stop off point for Kentish travellers. **Leeds Castle** is a fortress associated with major misunderstandings. These range from people travelling to the wrong part of the country to visit it (so we are told), to the more fatal error of a lord's gatekeepers mistakenly firing upon the royal party, angering the king who then beheads him.

Its beauty however is always undoubted, and the castle itself becomes traditionally handed over as part of the royal dowry for ex-Queens to keep on the death of their husband as some consolation. As such, the place becomes associated with the illicit marriage of Henry V's widow and Owen Tudor.

It's a place of royal honeymoons as much as of war. Edward III's defensive improvements certainly don't spoil its look. Thankfully, you're unlikely ever to need to swim under fire to get inside it. Which is just as well given the swans.

With the French raids, more castles start to be built along the southern coastal areas. That's especially true after some of the great military victories, when individual nobles have some cash to throw around and would rather live without fear of losing it again to a band of salty Norman sea dogs on a day trip. Thus in our travels we can come across some wonderful new homes that double as fortifications.

An amazing example of this is at **Scotney**. The site itself has already been occupied, but in the 1370s a new moated defensive structure is being put up lower down the hill. We're not entirely convinced it would prove a massive obstruction to a major army, though a raiding party might balk enough to move on to an easier target. What's certainly true is that in addition to providing some of the mod cons of our era in a quasi-manor house building, wandering around the outside cannot fail to impress with the striking beauty of the place, especially in summer.

There is more to the south east than just Kent though. Travelling through Essex, we suggest you aim to pass through the town of **Colchester.** While nowhere near as impressive as its Roman forebear, it does have the advantage of not one but two monastic establishments in which to break your journey. The clunky antiquity of the castle gives it an endearing air. But the real reason to come is for its famous oysters. It's said a brewing argument about a creek where some of them grow even risks growing into a major spat with the Cinque Ports.

But let's now turn our gaze further out west. You may have been impressed by Canterbury, but if anything the cathedral at **Salisbury** is even more imposing. The main part of the building is under a century old, and the spire is only right now being completed. It'll still need some more work on it, and you can watch the architects themselves supervising the work on the scaffolding in the 1370s that you suspect they might never get round to taking down. The wall around the close is also a recent build, though the stones themselves come from the original cathedral, now a memory ripped from time and the landscape over at Old Sarum. At 404 feet it is one of the tallest structures in the entire country, pointing directly up to Heaven. The nearby hall, with its minstrels' gallery, makes for a cosy venue if you are invited to dine socially and can't quite wrangle an invite into the bishop's palace.

Further along veering to the north, you might seek to break your journey at **Lacock Abbey**. It sits on the banks of the River Avon, and is properly speaking a nunnery. As such in the unlikely eventuality that you are a female traveller, obviously under escort, this provides an example of the sort of halting point you might seek to aim for when mapping out your route. As Augustinians they don't withdraw entirely from the world, but neither do they run a hostelry for general convenience. Gruff bestubbled types will not likely make it through the front door. There's a hedge and ditch, and later a wooden wall, if you want to play the rake and risk provoking the royal wrath: the abbess has friends.

Instead of heading north from Salisbury, you might be heading south and abroad. In that case you'll want to take ship at **Southampton**, perhaps the land's third port after London and Bristol. The town is walled, to a point ... but not enough to prevent any French raider from sailing into town and plundering the place as the defences don't yet cover the waterfront. The castle in the northern part of town is not frankly imposing enough to dissuade and will still need some major work on it. Still, we prefer it over Portsmouth if only because that location gets sacked twice by the French. It's also from this fort that Henry V effectively declares war and then embarks on his celebrated campaign.

Artwork by Philip Brannon, courtesy of Southampton City Art Gallery

Thankfully, despite an early French attack, much of Southampton survives, including the town houses of the merchants trading with distant Gascony. Armies leaving for Brittany and the south will need to be supplied, and this port will provide much of it. The walling - once completed – provides a reassuring and solid backdrop, and the old Bargate entranceway is worth a viewing. There's a weekly market and an annual fair. Less well-off travellers should head for God's House, which is a monastic building with accommodation available. Thanks to the Franciscans there is now piped water in the town.

Late visitors should note that parts of the old town have survived the ravages of war, and in particular the medieval walls remain extensive if at places somewhat restored. Sadly, the Archaeological museum is no longer there, but a walk with illustrative plaques does exist around the town.

SeaCity Museum provides a useful maritime overview of the port through the ages, while the City Art Gallery has a wide collection covering six centuries.

Visitor details can be found at www.southampton.gov.uk in the leisure section, including information on exhibitions.

The road to the hinterland takes us north east to **Winchester**. This is another important cathedral city. Its royal connections date back to Saxon times, but more recently it's also the site where   Henry III established his round table. The royal apartments in the castle were devastated by a fire as recently as 1302, and there's no evidence that they are ever going to be refurbished, though Henry IV will marry in the city and the wedding feast in Wolvesy Palace (where the bishop lives) is a must-have invite. Also, if you are looking for somewhere to send your son for a good education, Winchester College is founded in 1382.

Back to the coast now and head west into **Poole**. The town is of relatively recent foundation, but is admirably sited and prospering well. By the Low Season, it's a designated staple port for wool exports, has its own annual fair (soon to be doubled), and manages its own affairs. Though only hosting a few hundred inhabitants, it's important enough to attract the attention of French raiders twice, not that you might think it from the thatched roofs that lend this place on a misty dawn the feel of a half-forgotten fishing village. But it's as an example of burgeoning urbanity that Poole draws us, a town on the make with aspirations and growing pride. Go down to the wool warehouse in particular, which is by the dockside. The town cellars form an imposing building that speaks eloquently of the power of trade.

Artwork by Graham Smith MA (RCA) (c) Poole Museum

Late visitors can still see the town cellars, which act as a local history centre sited next to the town's museum. The latter also incidentally hosts an Iron Age log boat. Access is free, but note is closed Sunday mornings and (in the past) all day Monday – we recommend you check before visiting.

Poole Museum runs a twitter account, http://twitter.com/poolemuseum, and is also on Facebook at http://facebook.com/poolemuseum.

Also in town is Scaplen's Court, a medieval town house. This is often open for events, and during August. We suggest accessing the council website, http://www.boroughofpoole.com.

Central and Eastern England

The South may host the nation's capital and many of its old ports, but there's a lot more to the country. Coventry will be on the itinerary of many a serious merchant thanks to its wool trade, and in particular the famous and durable local blue cloth. The market is sited by the abbey gates.

Another monastic site in the area is Sandwell Priory, over in West Bromwich.

(c) Sandwell Council

The priory was built between 1190 and early 1300's. It was founded by the d'Offini family but completed after the extinction of the male line when West Bromwich Manor was shared out between the de Marnhams and Devereaux. The prior has just had a new chamber built. There's a fishpond and dovecot, used to support those in the infirmary. Don't expect a rigidly-enforced rule here as the bishop has told monks off for such faults as wandering around in normal clothes, roughing up their leaders, and for mismanaging their estates. There's also a long-running dispute with the Abbot of Shrewsbury which has led to one abbot being shot in the arm with an arrow.

A new Manor House was built as recently as 1290. Pop by to see Walter Devereaux, who in 1369 is a liege of Hugh de Bohun and is an old friend of ours.

Late visitors will sadly find little on the site today beyond rubble. The Priory as it happens was closed down a decade before the Dissolution; the buildings were not spared.

However, those interested in the history of the area can visit another site instead. A recent public acquisition from this period is Manor House, an important timber framed survival with a very early great hall. It's open for organised visits and for special events from July to September: more details are on http://www.sandwell.gov.uk/museums.

Leicester is a Midlands town with an unusual amount still standing from Roman times. The old baths complex, or what's left of it, reminds visitors of the town's broken heritage. Much more recent is the impressive new hospital of the Newarke and the town's burgeoning guildhall. The market area takes up the south east corner of the walled town, and leather is a local speciality worth checking out. The town has a minor fort: it's hard to credit that the powerful de Montfort family of rebels were ever associated with it.

By contrast, the fortress of **Warwick** provides an imposing oversight over its walled town. This is held by the de Beauchamps who seem to revel in trying to outdo each other in elevation. It's also where Edward II's favourite, Piers Gaveston, was grabbed and murdered a few years ago. A fine quarter of the town itself is the area around the Norman gateway and its associated chantry chapel; right next to it is a cluster of fourteenth century buildings that make up the home of the guilds. See if you can find the small Master's Garden for a secluded moment to yourself.

Northampton may not have such a famous castle (though it is still important), but it's a significant town all the same. Shoemaking has been associated with the place since at least the early thirteenth century. If it's looking a bit run down, it's because it's not fully recovered from being sacked after a revolt against the King also a century ago.

Of its churches, take a look at that of the Holy Sepulchre, built by a crusading knight and based on that of Jerusalem. Just out of town is one of the dozen Eleanor's Crosses, marking the overnight resting place of the body of Edward I's queen as she was brought back to London.

Nottingham has a far grander history, in part because of its associations with the legend of Robin Hood (increasingly becoming popular in our time), but also because the castle that dominates the hill top has so lately played an important part in the country's history. It was by gaining secret entry to the castle that Edward III seized control of the throne and grabbed and executed the regent, Mortimer.

But not all travellers will be in the heart of the Midlands. Some will be following the tracks up to the east coast. In such cases, **Ely** may be a crucial stop as the imposing summit of its landmark cathedral can draw travellers to it from far across the Fens. Well, it used to! Only a few years ago it came crashing down. The disaster has led to opportunity as a remarkable new octagonal tower is being raised in its place.

The marshes dictate much of the local economy – you surely must partake of the local delicacy of eels during your stay. It's not a packed urban scene, with orchards providing fresh fruit when in season. The city is a significant trading entrepôt so chances are you can get your wares at this watery crossroads – flints, timbers, canvas, local tiles and stone for carving, Ely-wound rope, or lead and wax from Boston.

Stamford we have already encountered in passing thanks to a dispute at the universities, where students and scholars decamped for a brief while to set up a new establishment. For such a small place it has a remarkable number of hospitals and churches, best explained by its situation on the Great North Road as well as on the River Welland. One, Grey Friars, is where the Black Prince's widow will be buried. In the fifteenth century, the wool trade will shift further east, but for now there is still also a clique of rich merchants acting as patrons to the church and to the poor. It's a significant enough location to draw the Great Council as a meeting place.

Those travelling north can split their route. Heading to the Wash takes you to the port of **Boston**. If Ely's tower helps people navigate on the marshes, the tower of Boston's church of St Botolph's – the Stump – is being built up as the dominant landmark for those heading out to see over these flat windy lands. A hundred years ago Boston was perhaps the second richest port in the country; in the fourteenth century, Boston is named a wool staple, confirming its wealth. But that trade is shifting, and the river is silting up. Enough of it remains navigable for it to stay a fishing town, but the great cogs can no longer make it all the way upriver. The glory days that paid for the feasts at the fine guildhall are gone.

Still, put the guildhall on your map. It's unusual, because it's made of brick – a design that Lincolnshire seems to be leading the way in. At the end of the Low Season on the edge of town, Sir John Hussey is building a manor house with a sturdy tower made of the same fabric. Up in the north of the county, Tattershall Castle is too. We're not sure using this strange and expensive status symbol fabric will ever catch on.

You know where you are with stone and that's certainly true if you take the land route north via **Lincoln**. That city, of Roman foundation, still has many of its old Norman era buildings that are as solid today as when they were first put up. It's past its heyday though and is no longer the third city of the kingdom that it was in the last century. But you wouldn't think that on first catching sight of the cathedral on the hill's summit, whose main tower has a huge spire that some claim as the tallest in the world. It dwarfs mighty Salisbury but much of it's wooden so perhaps that's cheating, and sometimes it looks a little unsafe to our eyes. Inside the building, look for the Rose Window and the fourteenth century carvings in the choir and the bosses up above you. Nearby, there are the twin symbols of the castle, and the bishop's palace that's the headquarters of the country's largest diocese. Down at the bottom of the hill at river level, catch a glimpse of the Fossdyke – some say it's Roman in origin, but in any event it's been a major canal since the twelfth century linking the city with the nearest major river, the Trent. It needs some work doing on it.

Turning away from the route north, the east coast plays host to some of the country's important ports. **Norwich** has at its heart a strong Norman keep and a recently-constructed friary. Look to King Street and Dragon Hall for an example of the fifteenth century entrepreneurial spirit – Robert Toppes has constructed a great store room and show room. Obviously there's a Guildhall to visit, as well as Stranger's Hall if you get an invite. The city's importance stems from the neighbouring counties being the centre of worsted cloth manufacture, while the town itself faces onto the North Sea allowing for trade with the Low Countries and the Hanse. Count the churches and you'll get a feel for the wealth in this place.

Contrast that with **Great Yarmouth**, which in scale is by far England's biggest port, and home to some of the greatest ships thanks to its naval builders. Its wealth is founded on its important herring fisheries, and remains an issue of considerable argument with the Cinque Ports over who has administrative rights – it's often come to blows and some say to actual piracy. That hasn't stopped the locals from edging more and more into the southern trade as Cinque harbours silt up.

Lynn is another port like Boston that opens onto the Wash. Originally four Lynns that were scattered along a river, the building of a church focused attention on the western settlement and confirmed the role of the local bishop. The Holy Trinity Guild and the Hanse guild buildings are home to some of the increasingly important players. Ships leave here to trade as far away as Iceland, provoking some diplomatic problems with the King of Denmark since they are breaking a monopoly, while showing how far local merchants are prepared to go. Consider Lynn coxswains if you are looking for participants in a risky trade venture; the roughest might even be up for a bit of white slavery.

Ipswich, sometimes called the Port of Orwell after its river, takes us back into the land of wool traders. It has significant trading contacts with the Baltic, and like its Norfolk counterparts relies on ship building and the local wool trade, benefiting from being accessible by river at some distance nearer to producers in the hinterland. If you are tracking down a port with a difference we would recommend rather **Dunwich**. The story of this town is a solemn tale of the temper of fate. For centuries it was a great and wealthy community. But over the course of several decades, gales had smashed into the town and mauled its waterfront. Then, recently, in 1328, a great storm shattered the coast, swamping buildings but more critically sweeping the shingle across the entrance to the port. With ships no longer able to enter the harbour, trade has shifted to other ports. Yet more markedly has been how since time immemorial the sea has been eating away at the land. Houses, churches and abbey buildings have been sucked away by gale-tossed currents. Visit this town before it sinks finally and irredeemably beneath the waves, leaving its bells to toll hauntingly in the depths.

Dunwich is famous for its saint, Felix, and is a pilgrimage site in its own right. But two far more celebrated ones lie inland. The first is at **Walsingham**, where the Franciscans are adding their own friary to the existing Augustinian one. The site's of international importance thanks to a set of visions that appeared to a Saxon noblewoman, where the Virgin Mary instructed her to build a replica of the house of the Annunciation. There's a village to cater for pilgrims' wants. The other site is at **Bury St Edmunds**, whose monastery holds the remains of a Saxon king martyred by the Vikings. It's also the place where the barons agreed to the Magna Carta project. The power in the town is the Abbot and there's a lot of strife about that fact given the growing wealth from wool. Some of the town even now still shows the scars from rioting in 1327.

The Centres of Learning

Two towns are important sites for reasons of trade in thought and learning. Oxford has been developing halls of residence since the town riots in the thirteenth century, leading to distinct colleges starting with Balliol and Merton (1264). Exeter was founded for students coming from the south west (1314). Oriel was set up ten years later. Since then, Queen's is established in 1341 by the Queen's Chaplain, and New College in 1379. Lincoln College is founded in 1427 by its bishop, probably on the back of fighting Lollards who had so vexed a previous generation of scholars. In 1437, All Souls is founded in memory of Henry V and the dead of Agincourt, and Magdalen in 1448. So there is an increasing opportunity for students who wish to improve their qualifications. Learning is predominantly by lectures, though a library is built in the 1440s. Study can begin at quite an early age. Starting with grammar and logic, and moving onto arithmetic, geometry and music, students are tested by debating with more senior students, with final exams with the masters. Some masters then progress to specialist study in divinity, canon and lay law, or medicine, and become doctors. Students are registered with their master (matriculation) and passes at various degrees recorded.

Cambridge is your other choice in England, and has perhaps a slightly less ecclesiastical feel and more of a country hall taste architecturally. It too is shifting out of church buildings and private accommodation and into special halls. Peterhouse was founded in 1284, and King's Hall (1317) set up by Edward II to train civil servants. Since then there's Michael House (1324), University Hall (1326, renamed Clare Hall 1338), Pembroke (1347), Gonville Hall (1348), Trinity Hall (1350), Corpus Christi (1362), Magdalene (1428), Buckingham College (1428), God's-house (1437), King's (1441), and Queens (1448). As the University Hall case shows, it wouldn't surprise us if some of these names change again over time, if indeed all of these colleges survive. King's is a marvel and has an old fashioned monastic beauty to it, extending to a remarkable chapel that work has just started on: we suspect it will be beautiful when it's finally completed from what we've seen of the plans, with designs for the largest fan vault in the world. If you are looking for something older, drop round by the Round Church, or Church of the Holy Sepulchre near the river front, which has a peculiar and endearing quality to its form.

The North and its Marches

The North of England may feel like it's on the edge of the civilised world, but that's no reason why you should avoid the home comforts. Trade routes run easily along the coast and along the main road routes supplying your essentials; the only areas where you may have to rough it are when on garrison duty in Scottish outposts.

Let's start in the north west. **Bury Castle** provides us with an example of how the gentry used to live. In essence they would protect themselves in a simple manor house, with sturdy walls and quite possibly a moat. Now, in this case the building itself is being rebuilt by an important Lancashire figure just after the close of the Low Season, on the site of a moated building perhaps going back to the previous century. While it's dated to just after the closing year of this tome, the later rebuild still provides us with a pointer as to how something a little less imposing than a full blown frontier fortress garrisoned by an Earl would look. It sits next to a village.

Artist Graham Sumner, (c) Bury Council Museums Service

Bury Castle is no longer extant, and this includes the subsequent rebuild represented above. Late visitors may still see some archaeological elements of the latter in the town centre, which take the form of significant exposed wall foundations. The tourist information centre has a leaflet on the castle available for visitors.

Radcliffe Tower dates from 1403 and is a bit more substantial. It's a survivor of an older hall that was pulled down in the nineteenth century.

The town website is at http://www.bury.gov.uk, which also contains information on visiting the art gallery.

Something a little more menacing lies at Shotwick. This is an old motte and bailey site overlooking a ford on the River Dee, topped by a stone keep, and with the motte surrounded by a ditch that fills at high tide. The original castle dates back to Norman times and was built to keep the Welsh out. That's since changed; it's now become the centre of a royal game park.

Friends with the Black Prince? It's to Shotwick that he might invite you hunting deer in 1353. If he really likes you, he might give you a full time job managing it. Don't worry, the Welsh won't invade so it's a simple management job these days. Enjoy the ornamental ponds and gardens.

Reconstruction by Tim Morgan, (c) Cheshire West and Chester Borough Council

Shotwick sadly is another site for the archaeologists to interpret. Late visitors can see mounds but nothing else. Still, it lasted longer than a number of the privately-held small castles from its era thanks to its royal connections. Given the lack of stone, which was robbed out by the eighteenth century, the artwork above required considerable investigative research in archives of limited detail and the dock is increasingly speculative. However, the key areas of doubtful archaeology including the keep have been avoided thanks to a sagacious choice of which angle to paint the view from.

More rewarding for visitors in the current century is a trip to Chester; we recommend the council's tourism section on its website at http://www.cheshirewestandchester.gov.uk/ and starting with the Grosvenor Museum.

More detailed information on the county's history site by site can be found in the online series Revealing Cheshire's Past (q.v.), and in back issues of the Council's Archaeological Service news letters. Tim Morgan is a freelance illustrator who has also worked for Cadw and for English Heritage.

You might have to put up with the odd unexpected guest passing through on official business on the way to the city of Chester. That is the domain of the Black Prince. It's in the time of Richard II the site of intrigue, pillaging and battle; dangerous turf so steer clear. It's also from Glendower's time a bad place to be if you're Welsh. From around 1403, visiting Welshmen have to enter the city unarmed, and in groups of no more than three. Resident Welshmen are forced to leave. Any caught at night risk death. We hope these laws are swiftly revoked as soon as the crisis passes. But if not Welsh, then do definitely take the time to go shopping along the covered arcades. The largely Roman city walls are worth a walk for the exercise, with a commanding view of the area. Work is ongoing on the choir stalls in the Benedictine Abbey, where you can also see the shrine of Saxon princess St Werburgh. But our favourite is when crossing the Dee Bridge. Chester is a frontier town, so this is the point where you are leaving the Kingdom behind and entering Wales – even if only for a bite to eat.

Over on the east coast, you'll possibly be heading for the port of Kingston-upon-Hull. It is admirably sited on the Humber and the river mentioned in its name. The name itself is quite a new one – within living memory it was still called Wyke, before being purchased by the monarch. It's still on the make and a community being built, much of it from local brick (even the new church), and with the de la Pole family very much in the lead. Fishing is very important for the village but as the new guildhall suggests, increasingly so too is trade.

You might though go slightly off the beaten track and be aiming for a more central route, taking in a trip to some mining interests around Derbyshire. Here our recommended port of call is Haddon Hall. Once a small Norman fort, this fine rural house has its own chapel, which from the Low Season has an admirable selection of wall drawings; you can get to them off the central courtyard. The building has a backdrop of rolling hills and a gentle stream, with a deer park nearby. Look out on the nearby village of Nether Haddon and its increasingly abandoned fields. As stopovers go, it's a lot less of a grinding climb than at Peveril Castle and is both rather less exposed and more homely, though this latter has the benefit of some notable views over the rugged Peak District once you make it to the wind-battered top.

Yorkshire is a great northern county containing a number of impressive sites, including a number of mighty abbeys such as Fountains and Rievaulx, both imposing and welcoming stopping off points, and smaller way points such as Byland whose tile floors remind us of an earthy stained window, or Roche with its quality stone quarry just outside of Rotherham.

Beverley on the other hand is famous for its minster. Work's ongoing but will finish by the Low Season. It's a popular attraction thanks to the miracles done by its founder, Bishop John. The town itself is less impressive, and the burghers have certainly scrimped on their city defences which have a Dark Ages minimalist feel to them. You'll have to increasingly hold your nose to as the brick and tile factories pollute the environment and encourage people to rip down the fruit trees. Despite the unpleasant environment it's quite large, with a Flemish community, and has its own grammar school.

You'll really be wanting though to press on to linger at York, which has long been one of the most important cities of England from Roman through Viking to modern times. Contrast its walls with Beverley's palisade and you know on entry this is a place of some significance. Note the gateways are locally called Bars, which might lead to confusion at night time. The city's dominant feature is the massive Minster, seat of the Archbishop and where Edward III recently married. It's renowned for its Mystery Plays. There are a number of churches, abbey buildings and a leper hospital, as well as a large and varied selection of merchants' houses and guild halls. It's probably the richest city in the country outside of London, trading as far as Germany and Scandinavia, and also acts as the administrative capital of the north.

If York is the capital of the north, the front line with the Scots is headquartered at Durham. This city perches on a hill almost surrounded by the River Wear. It's the domain of the Prince Bishop, who enjoys a high degree of autonomy – a detail best remembered if you have had run-ins with his men in the past. The powerful-looking cathedral, mostly Norman, is the resting place of St Cuthbert, whose shrine you must see, but historians will also be drawn by the tomb of the Venerable Bede. The presence of the river has encouraged mills, and with it industry so it's also a working city. Make some allowances as Robert the Bruce burned the place down, and it will be getting a town hall very soon.

On the cusp of the territory of the Scots, you're likely to be interested in visiting the great frontier castles. Begin with Warkwork. The castle rests on a hill in flat countryside, so is a prominent landmark in the area. It sits at the end of the village. You'll spot it even more readily when the keep, currently under construction, is completed.

The exit from the village to the north takes you through a gatehouse and across a bridge: you'll see the symbol of the Percys, the local magnates who are taking over this turf, marked out.

Dunstanburgh along the coast is one of a handful of imposing littoral fortresses. It's slightly unusual in not being held by a Percy; it's a royal castle. Looking at it we're not sure if it's been built more for show than for defence. There are two huge towers forming the gateway that look as if they've fallen from a giant's pocket, but it's simply too massive for its garrison and some points look exposed. It's also easily bypassed by any invading Scots. Still, it has its own harbour so it might prove a convenient disembarkation point if a storm brews. Turn up after the main building work is done in the 1380s and you can see a flagship statement of royal interest in this part of the world.

Bamburgh on the other hand is of far greater antiquity, a royal seat from the times of the first barbarian invaders. Latterly, it has proven a consistent anchor in the defensive chain in the north, facing the threat of numerous Scottish sieges. It's the King's castle, so you'll likely find house guests are unwelcome and have to stay in the village - unless you happen to be a Scottish royal prisoner.

Alnwick though is the heartland of the Percys. Their castle here predates them, and they've only been here a generation, but they are quick to make their mark. With their building works, this is becoming another critical border fortress. Perhaps that's one reason why Warkworth is more of a preferred residence for the family and where you're more likely to head to if coming up to visit. This is probably just as well, as the place draws rampaging Scots on at least two occasions in the fifteenth century and it's certainly not the most obvious place to be, especially if you can't get admission through the gates.

Newcastle is set to become the most northerly staple town. Proximity to the Scots has made it too often reliant upon its sturdy defences. That may increasingly shift now that Berwick has been captured, perhaps the one enduring legacy of the long drawn out and clearly failing attempt to integrate Scotland. That frontier town was Scotland's premier port and hugely important as a generator of tax revenue. For now at least, it's in English hands and the eastern archway of the frontier. Its counterpart in the west is Carlisle. This triple gated town has a weekly market and an annual fair. Its trade is in part focused on export to Scotland and Ireland. The region is pretty isolated and occasionally subject to raids, and on top of that burned down at the end of the thirteenth century, so don't expect too glamorous a conurbation. Still, it provides a base from which enterprising merchants can offer to supply English garrisons in occupied Scotland. Don't trust the defences too much.

Out West and the Welsh Marches

Travellers to outlying parts might instead choose to aim for the Celtic fringe. The Severn estuary bisects the old territories of West Wales (Cornwall and to some extent Devon) from Wales proper. Let's turn first to the extremity of England.

Plymouth is an old fishing town, but also a key embarkation point for pilgrims travelling overseas. If you have time to explore, we advise travellers to head for Exeter. It's an important town but no longer the port it once was, thanks to a local noble building a weir across the river. Nevertheless, even if ships can no longer unload directly into the heart of the city, wool continues to be exported and wine carried back. The marshy ground is beginning to be drained, and the power of the waste water harnessed by the construction of mills to help with the wool processing industry. Fresh water by comparison is piped in via underground cuts.

You may enter into town via the narrow bridge across the Exe, built over a century ago. It hosts a chapel so if you've had a narrow escape during a testy sea voyage, this may be your first opportunity to pray in thanks for having arrived safely. Whether you're invited into one of the merchant's homes during your stay, or simply get to appreciate the Guildhall, you'll quickly start to sense where the money lies. This helps explain why the city has so many parish churches nestling within its walls. Of particular interest is St Olave's which is an ancient relict. It was built by Harold Godwinson's mother for her husband, before the Conquest, and named after a recently-converted Scandinavian King. It gets redecorated at the end of the fourteenth century, so you can see the carving being done of the scourging of Christ during your visit.

It would be a major omission to spend all your time in the south west stuck in one town when the countryside in this part of the country has so much to offer. We have to point you in the direction of England's third largest city, Bristol. It's such an important place and will be a vital stop if you're trading in these parts, especially in wines from Gascony and Iberia. Its fishermen are doughty and head off west into strange and distant lands of rumour; don't try to press them on where they sail to as we hear they guard their far-off fishing grounds and their secret drying and salting landfalls jealously. Perhaps as some murmur there really is some new found land, out west. But for the tourists, we instead suggest you head inland and base yourself in Wells, a cathedral city that also enjoys healing springs (whence its name). The main business in town is clearly ecclesiastical, and equally obviously the second biggest relates to wool and cloth. The latter is rather important because in the fourteenth century there are major issues with the oversized main tower, requiring serious reconstruction work during your stay that needs financing. Happily, the West Front with its army of divine statues survives to impress. The recently-completed chapter house and cloisters also offer a peaceful retreat, and a lot of work is ongoing with the quires. Look out in particular for the spectacular stained glass windows showing the genealogy of Christ. From around 1390, the Cathedral hosts an intriguing clock, a rarity as well as for its design - every quarter of an hour, knights dash out. Next door, the bishop's own fortified palace dates from King John's time, and a stroll round the gardens as well as the halls is worth a detour.

In 1348, the vicars move into a street just off the side of the Cathedral, which runs up to a Hall where they communally eat and to which then is added a chapel. Each house serves one vicar, with enough window space to allow them to study, plus a toilet, and a bedroom. Visitors at the end of the Low Season can still find them occupied. Who knows if in later years they'll still be lived in, a direct living link to the time of the Black Death!

A number of the English towns dotted in the vicinity of the Welsh frontier feature prominently in the struggles for supremacy in the fourteenth and fifteenth centuries. That's no reason not to visit them without being accompanied by an army though. Gloucester has an important abbey and is probably in the top ten wealthiest towns in the land, though increasingly in the shadow of Bristol. The burial of Edward II in the abbey has, for now, kept the town on the map. Shrewsbury has the unfortunate distinction of being where Harry Hotspur gets killed by Henry IV in a major bloodbath. Stick to shopping in town. Worcester cathedral is the resting place of King John, who lost the royal lands in France and so was the first of his line who had to be buried in England (a loss currently being revisited). Don't seek to be put up in the castle, which is now run down and these days is a prison. Aim to be put up in Guesten Hall, a magnificent new timber building the bishop has constructed. Hereford might not have two saints like Worcester (it only has the one, and of more recent manufacture – Bishop Cantilupe), but it does have another useful resource. Go to the cathedral and see if you can access the library. The mappa mundi is a relatively recent drawing of the major cities of the world, and will prove a useful aid in planning your next holiday to one of the 420 towns set out on it.

You won't need too detailed a map to make your way from here into Wales. Given political developments and the Glendower Revolt we'll cover the area separately a bit later on. But for now let's follow the expeditions south, across the Channel and into France.

Normandy

The times are long gone since the people of Normandy associate themselves with their liege in London. The province is now the personal duchy of the heir to the French throne, and old English loyalties have long faded.

This makes the duchy admirable territory on which to campaign.

It is perhaps surprising that it doesn't happen more often. Gascony is a permanent battlefield. Flanders first draws the eye. Brittany provides a long campaign of opportunity. Normandy, easily sited opposite many English ports, should be a major target much earlier than it is. It certainly gets badly raided, and Edward III has a good rampage across it on the way to Crécy, but it's really only in the fifteenth century it becomes central to English ambitions and the war effort.

Let's focus on a couple of the main locations. Caen is the province's second city, famous for its stone that is exported for many an ecclesiastical building. Set in marshy surroundings, it hosts the old castle of William the Conqueror. The town itself is divided up by river branches. Worth visiting are the two old abbeys, the more westerly of which holds the tomb of the Conqueror himself.

Harfleur is the key location though. It's the major port of north western France, and the English will come to eye it as a potential second Calais for them. It has two gates, the Caltinant and Montivilliers, strong thick walls, deep wide ditches, and two strong towers on its coastal walls. It sits on the north bank of the Seine estuary, on the opposite bank of the smaller harbour of Honfleur.

The major location of tourist interest is upriver, Rouen. This is the old capital and a port in its own right, particularly focusing on tin and wool for its significant textile industry. It has a town hall, palace, and castle. Unique to northern Europe it additionally has a naval arsenal. As a centre of late English power, it's also the location to which Joan of Arc is brought, to face trial in the Archbishop's Palace and punishment in the main square.

The Cathedral deserves a visit. The Butter Tower, paid for by donations allowing people to eat butter during Lent, is very slowly going up. Head inside and marvel at the rich blue glass, reminiscent of the windows at Chartres. Keep an eye open for where Richard the Lionheart's heart lies buried.

On the other extreme of the coast, you definitely must see Mont St Michel. This fortress/town/abbey sits on a rock swept round by the shifting tides, so you'll need to time your visit carefully, and pay full heed to the locals on whether it's advisable to make a dash for the other shore. The place is essentially put under siege for thirty years. If it's in French hands it's largely because of du Guesclin, who practically single handedly takes on his opponents in a series of one-on-one maulings and holds the walls at a tricky moment. It's an important pilgrimage place thanks to its associations with the Archangel, so make sure you climb all the way to the top.

Brittany

There are in a sense two Brittanys. The east is French speaking and French-leaning, orientated by trade and by education towards the universities and bishops of the Loire. It's a place of traders, agriculture, and population. The west, however, has retained much of its Celtic past. The land is hillier, rockier, poorer, dependent on the sea, but more self-reliant and home to crenellated retreats, half-remembered saints and, magical legends.

The ducal capital is the city of Nantes, which does well out of the Loire tolls in salt and wines. The cathedral is a disappointment – they've only just begun building it at the end of the Low Season. The castle too is facing a major rebuild. The locals are a moody lot, probably because of the civil war which keeps planting them in the front line against a marauding army of one side or the other when all they want is to get on with their lives. Still, they are good with their cuisine. Go for the sea food and wash it down with cider.

Note that, along with Rennes, another important march town, you may find the French here a little strange. It's Gallo, a dialect as distinct as Norman or Picard.

Vitré is another frontier town, enjoying a thriving trade in cloth and canvas along its lively narrow streets. Mind as you descend the Rue de la Poterie as the familiar problem of houses with overhanging upper rooms means you'll need to watch out for unexpected presents from above. Beyond the thirteenth century walls, pass through the narrow St Pierre postern and aim for the Rachapt area. This was occupied while the town was under siege, and bought back from the English as a condition of the siege being lifted – hence the name.

By contrast its sister town, the fortress of Fougères has a more spacious air. This is a very wealthy place, and the home of a number of influential people. The castle here sits upon a major granite ledge and is exceptionally intimidating to the casual assaulter. The town is taken by a surprise attack by freelancing English soldiers in 1449. The booty is immense – it's the trashing of the richest frontier town. But the act triggers the final phase of the Hundred Years War.

Do note though that the defences only cover the castle itself and part of the local residencies. If a hostile force arrives during your stay, you will have to dash over to the castle for safety. On the positive side, being located where it is allows residents of the lower town access to the river, which is particularly key for tanners. The area is a major centre for cattle breeding and from it, leather. Head for the Place du Marchix and its pleasant buildings, or track down one of Brittany's few belfries (bats are very disappointed in this province).

Largoët is the castle of the town known as Elven. It sits in a huge woodland, and dates from the late fourteenth century. Some claim that its keep is the tallest in France, and while we've not had the opportunity to measure it, it looks like it's a strong candidate. The village itself is unremarkable.

Out west the scenary is striking and the shoreline treacherous. One place you might stop over at is Brest. This begins as a small fishing harbour but the war makes its fortunes. Thanks to its permanent English garrison it gains in importance and ends up as quite a significant town.

If you're after somewhere with some character, head instead for the town of Clisson. It's south east of Nantes on the cusp of the Loire lands. The whole place still carries a charm that the wars haven't spoiled. There's the covered market, and the two stone bridges across the gentle rivers that here meet. Looking down is the castle, held by a Breton knight who becomes Constable of France before defecting back, a microcosm of Brittany's tortured and tortuously personal politics.

Northern France

Some of the richest lands in France lie in the north, and by dint of the wars, some of the most strategically important. At the head of the list sits Calais. A harbour opposite the Cinque Ports, its capture provides an enduring foothold for English expeditions into either the Low Countries or France as opportunity presents. It becomes an important trading centre, and increasingly a mighty fortress with a reputation for strength across all of Europe. Of course there are the other long-term English garrison towns in the north: Cherbourg and Brest both provide residents with excellent opportunities to loot their neighbourhoods over several decades of military occupation. But neither of those has been colonised. Significantly, Calais is also a very English town as a decision is made at the outset to populate it with English settlers. It will thus even in due course send MPs to Parliament. Looking around you can see why it took so long to capture, with its surrounding marshes and rivulets adding to the double defences of the town and the castle, and the sandy soil hindering any attempts to tunnel. Critics by contrast say it costs far too much to garrison. See what you think.

If you want to get away from English tavern grub, head inland to Arras. Lodge at the abbey of St Vaast. You probably won't be able to enjoy the abbot's marvellous carpets, but it's better sited than the town on a busy market day. Sadly, the town's glory days as a centre for theatrical excellence have faded. Avoid Cambrai which is horrible and marshy and a tedious place to be stuck besieging.

Perhaps a better bet is Lille. Arras is Burgundian but thanks to the architecture, Lille properly feels it. The sturdy build of the Burgundian almshouses gives the place a distinct flavour. It's not as big as Tournai but perhaps these days a little easier to get to.

Flanders is a key battleground at the start of the War, and a major diversion for the French for some years into it. It's also a hugely important trading area. Visitors might be confused why it's part of France at all. In fact, the big nobles are French and the ordinary people are Flemish – certainly the further north and west you go, the more of a sense of divided loyalties you get.

Two of the key Flemish cities are Ghent/Gand and Bruges/Brugge. Both are highly populous, urbanised and urbane centres, with a highly politically conscious middle class with a sense of identity and awareness of their own unique interests. This is reflected in their buildings that display an ornateness and pride other towns simply cannot afford. Bruges is also coloured by its canals that open up into picturesque gardens and offshoot alleyways. Track down the peaceful almshouses, crane your neck at the church tower of Our Lady that's the tallest brick building in the world, and wander over to watch the work being done on one of the finest city halls anywhere. In Ghent, it's the Patershol district by the count's castle that you want to frequent.

There are too many Flemish towns to visit and in a fleeting visit you'll not do them justice. Many of them aren't front line territory during the war. Ypres/Ieper is one exception. Having been wrecked by a siege, it passes to Burgundian hands and its defences at least are repaired, even if the economy isn't. Sluys, as we have seen, is another.

But it would be a shame to miss out on a trip to Antwerp. Ships can moor just a hundred yards from the main market place, which is a real convenience. A small castle guards the centre of the town, overlooking the waterfront. What really dominates the town though is the cathedral. You're not going to appreciate it much until the Low Season, and it doesn't even then look as if it'll be finished for some time yet. But it's clearly going to end up as a sky-scratching alternative to the little chapel that used to be on the site. The builders are talking about building five huge spires but we'll believe that when we see the work begun.

A crowning moment

Down firmly in France proper, two cathedral cities should definitely be on your itinerary. Both are in the Champagne region, part of the royal estates. The first is Troyes. You're in for a son-et-lumière display in

1389 when the nave collapses and one of the major windows drops out. The stained glass that stays put, however, is a treat. Troyes is an important diplomatic town, as it's where the French royals run to when they lose Paris. It is where a deal is done to put Henry V on the throne of France after the French king dies; Rheims on the other hand is where that deal is undone.

As Jules Eugène Lenepveu portrays, it's to the traditional coronation site of Rheims that Joan of Arc travels with a large army to crown the Dauphin king. At a stroke, the claim of England's King Henry VI is undermined. There are now two officially-endorsed claimants.

Associated with the site across town is the Abbey of St Remy, which hosts the tombs of several important figures including Charlemagne's brother. The episcopal residence, the Palace of Tau, acts as the royal hotel during the coronation process and the site of the inaugural banquet. These are definitely events to try to get an invite to if you have friends at court. But they'll have to be extraordinarily powerful friends for a show as big as this.

Paris

Paris during the High and Mid Seasons is the largest and the richest city in northern Europe, with a population in the order of a hundred thousand people. It's a dreamy mirage of slender, tall wooden buildings crammed into errant streets over which their upper stories loom. It's a leading entrepôt and a second home to a dazzling array of countless nobles, but also a refuge for common folk eking out an urban living.

Note that there are no sewers until well into the Mid Season. The first thing you're likely as a visitor to encounter after sighting the rising spires of the city is the boundary stream that carries away the dumped effluent. There is a major paved thoroughfare running north-south, a rarity for these times. But otherwise the streets are an open sewer, the banks of the river muddy, the outskirts of town an ill-starred swamp. So it's not all glitter. Especially after a hundred years of war when there are wolves on the wintry streets.

But at the outset of the High Season, all is splendour. If you can, time your visit to coincide with a major royal event, such as a marriage. You might find children in the street in a stage scene pretending to be angels dangling from the sky, fountains sporting blue cloth and sprinkled with golden fleur-de-lys, fountains of claret and spiced wine, stages with heroic historic mock battles (though the history might be tweaked to honour the monarch), lanes lined with silk or tapestries hosting the music of organs, or even a large model castle with wildlife and fake beasts around it. A real treat might be to watch a tightrope walker coming down from the cathedral heights, performing acrobatic stunts and bearing candles as darkness falls.

The heart of the city is on the island; Notre Dame looms over the east, in the final stages of completion, while the west is taken by a royal palace, the Conciergerie. It's true that these places are remarkable for their size and contents, such as the table that's made of the largest marble slab in the world, or the impressive royal sideboard. But these are tourist traps; we recommend you narrowly focus first on the palace's Sainte Chapelle. This astonishingly beautiful chapel hosts a number of important relics bought from the French conquerors of Byzantium, housed in the most ornate of gold reliquaries.

South of the Seine is the university quarter, leading up to the Abbey of St Germain des Prés with its tombs of ancient Frankish kings. North of the river is the merchant's quarter. Let's head in that direction.

Cross the bridge (don't loiter: it'll collapse in 1407) and pass by the Châtelet, a garrison fort held by the governor, and head out to the lofty royal fortress of the Louvre. A lot of work is being done on this to make it much more inhabitable, which you probably won't get to see (and won't want to as it's also a gilded prison for noble captives), but you can at least admire the ghostly pale stone that lights up eerily under dim moonlight. Head back into town and aim for Les Halles. This is the main market area, particularly for foodstuffs. The eastern part of the city is skylighted by the mass of the Bastille fortress, which forms the right hand hinge of the walls. You can find the royal chapel nearby, and also another royal palace the St-Pol. Its courtyard opens up onto the Seine. This is where the horrendous 'dance of the burning men' takes place.

Some claim that outside of Paris, the locals are parochial and they don't like outsiders, let alone foreigners – and this before the war even begins. Paris is a bit different. It's the hub of the kingdom that draws people in: students to the university, plaintiffs and defendants to the courts, nobles to the royal court. Right now in the High Season the city is flourishing. Dark days are coming that will eclipse it for a while; enjoy the cultural glow.

The Loire and Centre

South of Normandy, key battlefield turf lies in the Duchy of Maine. In particular, its city of Le Mans with its timbered and slate roofed houses is worth a detour, as well as the cathedral whose slow construction has resulted in a compendium of architectural styles. Pass on through and head into the lower Loire area proper.

Begin by breaking your journey at Asnières. It's a very pleasant stop with a Romanesque bridge over the Vègre, a courthouse, but in particular the church. Here the frescos set out in colourful motif the early life of Jesus.

Pouancé is Anjou's gateway into Brittany. Its castle is one of the largest in the area. It's also an important tax post. On the French side of the border, the authorities are experimenting with different rates of tax for salt, which is an important local industry. On the Breton side the revenue is largely raised by the Duke as a local landowner selling the material. But what that means is that it encourages smuggling across the border to avoid the tax take. Don't get caught is our advice.

The key city in this area is Angers. It's an important city and culturally its reach stretches into eastern Brittany. We begin with a trip to the castle.

The first thing you'll appreciate is the geography. The fortress, like the town, sits on the banks of the lower Maine, just above the point where it feeds into the Loire. The present castle was in large part constructed by St Louis, and a glance at its walls and moated area show how defendable it is. As it turns out , it won't need to be quite so well. Lucky Locals.

Once you enter into the fortification you might be surprised to spot the work that's going on to make the place more of a residence than a grim garrison.

There's a chapel at the heart of the castle, providing a rather more convenient location for devotion for residents than traipsing over to the cathedral across in the city proper.

Where there's a cathedral there's a bishop, and where there's a bishop, there's often a palace. With the presence of an important school in town it's just possible you might be able to get access to the Episcopal residence. If circumstances permit it and you're waiting for an audience, or simply attending a function, wander over to the fireplace. Tucked away by it is a curious inscription in mirrored Latin: we think it's an encouragement to drink but see what you make of it. Also worth a quick visit if you're heading west is a stop off at the hospital, which is a legacy from the days of the Angevin Empire and Henry II of England. Yes, there's a reason why that English dynasty had that name, and it's because they came originally from here.

Travelling east, your route will likely take you past Saumur. You're now in the heart of wine making country. The place is very much on the frontline in the desperate engagements around the time of the Siege of Orléans and its aftermath.

The town itself has somewhat improved since ancient times when the inhabitants lived in cosy caves. You might still be able to camp out in one if caught in bad weather.

Freshwater eels are a local delicacy, washed down with the excellent red wine.

You're starting to get into serious religious territory in this area. The town has a significant shrine to St John, a local hermit. Tours further east is associated with the important relics of St Martin, who shared his cloak with a beggar by cutting it in two (you'll see this image a lot in town), and the village of Candes-Saint-Martin is also part of that story.

But the most impressive religious site of all is the Abbey at Fontevrault, a little further up river. It's a huge complex, thanks to some impressive patronage. Richard the Lionheart, Eleanor of Aquitaine and Henry II all lie here in tombs topped with bright polychrome images of them at rest. This is the ancient burial place of the Kings of England when they owned large chunks of France centuries ago, before King John lost them. Only his heart and that of his son made it to this final resting place. Both nuns and monks serve here, including devotees from some of the greatest families.

Also in the vicinity, rather to the south west is the castle of Montreuil-Bellay. Its tale is an example of the impact of the war on the minor nobility. The viscount who owns it is one of those killed at Agincourt, without leaving a male heir. His daughter takes the territory with her as dowry. This at least brings outside wealth into the town, which acquires a school, a hospital and a tithe barn off the back of it. But it also leads to some significant fortifications needing building too.

Whether you are an historian or a French royalist, you really must put Chinon on your itinerary. Its long fortress used to be a key royal domain in Anglo-Angevin times. In particular, it's where Henry II died – a sordid end as he expires in fury at his sons for political betrayal. He is swiftly deserted by most of his retainers, and his corpse plundered to pay off debts. But in the Low Season it's become a key place for the court of the Dauphin, and it's to a first storey room in the castle that Joan of Arc comes to deliver her message. This is where the petty prince tries to hide his identity and have an imposter playfully assume his role, though Joan sees through this trick. Perhaps as you lean on the fireplace watching this you might be in a better place to judge whether it's thanks to a nudge from her guide, or having seen his noggin on a coin, but he takes it for more confirmation that she's on a mission for God. Enter via the gateway on the right.

North east of Chinon is the handsome castle of Ussé (left). It was once a Viking outpost. The latest castle is being rebuilt from ruins in the Middle Season. We are looking forward to the work being done on the gardens. It's a sleeping beauty.

The owner's son will marry the daughter of the King and his mistress, the famous Agnes Sorel. Sorel is associated with the incredible royal town of Loches in Touraine, whose castle brings together a remarkable range of architectural periods, from an early keep to an ultra-modern mini palace. This is where Joan of Arc returned triumphant after Orléans. It is wondrously beautiful.

Now leave Anjou well behind and head into the county of Blois. That town will be a key centre of operations for Joan of Arc, blocking English moves west from Orléans. Our focus is first drawn rather to an outlier.

Vendôme sits to the north on the River Loir (without an 'e'), with its castle peering down from its dominating hillside. Look down on the town's defences and pick out the Tour de l'islette, and the Porte St-Georges. From your lofty vantage point, you should also be able to make out the Convent, and Trinity Abbey.

And so as we head upwards towards the Loire Valley finally we find ourselves reaching the key city of the Low Season. Orleans sits astride the river, connecting east and west through its water traffic, and Paris and the south thanks to its critical bridge. It's a major centre for tolls and taxes. This makes it one of France's wealthiest cities, and the Sainte Croix cathedral rivals that of Notre Dame in Paris. Its university was established at the turn of the fourteenth century. In that age, you'll probably be drawn to the city for its learning or in passage; in the Low Season, bring armour.

Gascony

Whether trading or fighting, there's a very strong chance you'll spend some of your time in Gascony. It is after all the trigger of the war, a scene of pretty well non-stop fighting (even when there's an official truce), a base for freelance freebooting, and the pivotal point for much of England's import trade.

The key city is its capital, Bordeaux. Since the loss of England's old favourite wine producing region Poitou, this relic of the old Aquitaine empire has stepped up to the mark. We count five stages when the city walls have had to be expanded, making it the biggest city under the control of the King of England after London. Its position beside the broad Garonne means that sea going ships can dock right by the city walls to unload, while it commands the wine route so effectively that distant towns well beyond the reach of the King-Duke have to lobby the local government to get preferential deals over when their exports are allowed to sail.

The town is governed by a military seneschal and by a constable, but other than these most of the people running the place tend to be locals. Gascony's fortunes will wax and wane over the coming years, but Bordeaux will continue to flourish for as long as the English link is there for the city to supply its markets. A word for the wise though: avoid lending any money to support the local war effort. There's a real shortage of cash and the early part of the conflict is only maintained by scrimping, deferred repayment, loyalty, big promises and considerable luck.

Exploring the city, you'll probably be drawn to the cathedral. This is where Eleanor of Aquitaine's first marriage took place ... to the King of France, before she united her duchy's fortunes to England's. Work is continuing on this building until surprisingly late. The separate bell tower spans the final transfer of power and is associated with the saintly last archbishop of the old regime before the French conquest. As you explore this and other religious monuments, you'll begin note a distinctive English flavour with a preference for Nottingham alabasters.

Rather more impressive ancient statues can be seen on the incredible Piliers de Tutelle. This is a Roman temple, slender and lofty Corinthian columns supporting arches all set on a high platform. It's a wonderful sight: let's hope it survives future regimes, and the Roman amphitheatre along with it.

The main religious building lies just out of town in an old swampy area. It's the Basilica of St Seurin. The patron saint, a particularly holy man in late Roman times, was buried here along with his only marginally less holy predecessor/successor. You can see the fine sarcophagus inside the main building. As a result it's become one of the top places to be buried anywhere in Europe, on a par with Alyscamps just outside of Arles. Charlemagne's peers in the epic Song of Roland are said to rest in its grounds. The site is easy to find. You can spot it across the watery fields by its stocky bell tower, but also from the direction of traffic. Bring a small donation.

The major towns under Bordeaux's control swing back and forth as time passes. One worth reviewing for your itinerary is Blaye which is further down the river, on the northern bank, and as such a key gateway city. More consistently in English hands is nearby Bourg. Both are critical for commanding the lower reaches of the river trade and the route for reinforcement by sea. The fourth of the important B's lies at the other end of the province at the foot of the Pyrenees. Bayonne isn't a mighty fortress town but does enjoy the added attraction of quite a different culture, thanks to the Basques.

We hope you don't confine yourself just to the fortresses. The political situation may be extremely complicated, with the shifting loyalties of local lords as their enemies sign up to one side or another, and that makes for local wars of opportunity and power grabs. But the countryside is remarkable and many of the towns thoroughly deserve a visit. Top of the list is the garrison frontier town of Saint Emilion, an island besieged by quality vineyards. The town is also famous for its rock-hewn church, whose main chamber has been carved out of the solid hill by a shaky crusader with a penchant for foreign art. It can be found beside the cave of the hermit who gave his name to the town. The troglodyte theme is also carried across into the design of the town's main tower, which you access first by going underground. The town betrays its varying ownerships over the ages with a French royal tower, and the paintings in the main church. If business with all the wine dealers is getting a bit too much for you, nip off the high street and take a breather in the shade of the cloisters.

The Rest of France

We're not quite sure if the north of the Alps is any holier from the move, but these days the Papacy is clearly less Italian and more Gallic. The fourteenth century is the period of the "Babylonian Captivity" as popes first set up stall in a French town, then return there as a breakaway faction. Avignon becomes an important diplomatic and religious centre, and as the Popes settle down they begin to build. At Avignon's heart is the awe-inspiring and muscular bulk of the Palace of the Popes, which also serves as their head office. For instance it's where the chief court sits. If it has a fortress feel, it's with good reason, and occasionally popes will have need of protection, which is perhaps ironic given its role as a centre for so much diplomacy.

There's a major library there with literally hundreds of books. But see if you can get access to some of the private studies and chapels as the artwork is exquisite.

The town itself is also worth touring. Its wealth in some part comes from its celebrated bridge that spans the Rhône, dedicated to St Benezet whose principle claim to fame was starting the work with an impossible feat of manual labour after a vision told him to get the job started. There's a chapel dedicated there to him for the task he never got to see completed. Be careful when crossing it as the ground is slippery and people have disappeared over the edge.

Avignon itself is walled and houses a number of religious establishments. There are more across the river in the town of Villeneuve, which you can see from the summit of the rock. Villeneuve is a recent construction and a painfully visible reminder to cardinals that the French Kingdom sits right on their doorstep. Entry is through a lofty gateway for those prelates who prefer to base themselves on this bank and in the offices of the town's grand monasteries.

If you're not on an embassy or on a pilgrimage to see the Holy Father, then it's quite possible you've stepped out of Gascony and are on the move – or rampage – across the southern marches.

Narbonne is probably the furthest you're likely to get when campaigning. It's a town in decline thanks to flooding and the silting river. The arrival of the Black Prince might just add to the difficulties. The war has also encouraged builders to stop work on the cathedral, which was set to expand but requires the ancient wall to be pulled down first, and right now nobody is too happy with that prospect. The Archbishop's Palace is a serious piece of work though, and we recommend you keep your eyes peeled for the various pieces of Roman statuary scattered across town.

To the west into the hills, head for Lagrasse. It's a walled town on the banks of a narrow river noteworthy for its fine bridge, but in particular for its abbey. It's an important mother institution for many monasteries across this whole region, and a stroll in the cloisters or a view of the mural in the abbot's chapel are worth the detour.

Continue to head into the hinterland. A crucial stop is the frontier city of Carcassonne. Like Narbonne it's of Roman foundation, and many of the towers and walls date from those times. It was seized by the French Crown in the wake of the Albigensian Crusade, a period that has left many scars on this whole region. The main fortress was further built up, and a new town established on the far side of the river. It's this lower town that falls to the Black Prince during his expedition into this area: the massive defences of the old city elude him. If you are a more welcome guest, plump for a tavern as the count's residence is not much more than a small keep, although the view from the battlements is impressive.

Some at this point might wend their way south to try their chances in Iberia, starting with the civil wars in Castile. We certainly would encourage those visitors who do have the time to pass through the merchant houses of Barcelona, or along the pilgrim's trail though the Valley of Roncesvalles where Count Roland died in legend, over to Saragossa and on to Santiago de Compostela. From 1373, England and Portugal also enjoy a new-fangled alliance, building on the vital support given by English crusaders against the Moors. But that's an expedition for another day. Let's head back north into French frontier land instead.

North of Carcassone, we suspect you'll be drawn to Albi. Its cathedral is remarkable – it almost looks as if it's been moulded from a gigantic block of stretched clay. Beside it stands the bishop's fortress, the Berbie Palace, with its views over the bridge, the valley and the river Tarn. Alongside there's the Castelvieil and the Castelnau districts (old and new). Note the mills by the waterfront, and the busy dock. Saffron is an increasingly key mainstay of the local economy, but so too is the pastel trade that supplies blue dyes. Toulouse is beginning to threaten Albi's dominant position in the pastel export market, but for now the trade is brimming and extremely profitable. See if you can spot the fist-sized balls of dry pulp, or the end paste product on sale in the market. You're bound to get a solid profit if you bring a few of these back with you to any of the cloth weaving districts of northern Europe.

Many of the towns you'll come across in and around Gascony's borders are bastides, fortified settlements. One of the earliest and our recommendation is that of Cordes. It lies perhaps three fifths of the way between Bordeaux and the Mediterranean. The thirteenth century ramparts crown the summit of a major hill, so be prepared for a steep climb when you get there.

It's only been as recently as the 1320s that the Church has finally been able to overturn the Cathar influence here. That hasn't stopped the expansion of the town, and the fortifications are now a little more sprawling and confused as they have been rebuilt several times to catch up. The English front line draws up to just a couple of hills away, but bandits and brigands run ahead of it so do take care if here during the High Season and travel with an escort or in company. It's worth it if you do make the effort; the view from the market square is impressive, and there is a variety of craft shops.

Beyond the Contenders

Like Spain, some of the contenders' neighbours will see the fight spill over into their territory. One place that will see an awful amount of action is Scotland. We really strongly suggest avoiding taking tourist trips to this kingdom for much of this period. It's a place of terrible destruction, burning and massacre. As soon as any nice castle gets retaken by the Scots, they often deliberately wreck it so the English can't use it as a local base any more. Border areas are places of raid and ambush. You're not even safe behind walls at night, with many a castle captured by a surprise assault in the early hours.

The only plus side for the southerners is that after losing some key battles in the run up to the Hundred Years War, it revolutionises English tactics. It's the French who will have to suffer some horrific defeats based on mobility, missile power and dismounted knights.

If you've got no choice in the matter, plump for one of the larger garrisons, such as Stirling or Edinburgh. The local towns are larger and have more conveniences; the locations are more strategically important and therefore more likely to be prioritised for relief, supply and support; and with sturdier defences if things do go badly, you have a better chance of negotiating terms and marching out of there alive.

Only go to the Highlands and Islands in times of peace. They are attractive but the locals are scary, have huge swords, dress strangely, and scream at you in a language you won't understand.

We can say much the same about volunteering for military duty in Ireland. The area around Dublin is held by the Crown; the rest is open to feuds and ambushes. There are some interesting towns out there, for example grey lofty Cashel perched on its rock, or Dunluce that pinches out on a promontory and looks out onto the distant island where Robert the Bruce hid in his cave.

For somewhere more civilised – or at least feeling more familiar – head by sea for Cork in the south west. This is a small outpost of wealth and sewage, where you can embark a shipload of grain or beef. Alternatively, for a trading station with more of an Irish feel, head for the western enclave of Galway whose leading merchants are gradually taking over political control of the town: their interests lie in ensuring visitors like yourself, especially if trading, are protected.

There are also opportunities for mercenary work. But the rules of war are perhaps a little rougher should you get captured; the fortifications resemble what you'd find in the bottom of the garden; and the booty too often moo's rather than glitters. The island is also remarkably densely populated. So if you are going to go campaigning, we suggest you stick a little closer to the supply lines of your home comforts.

The last free areas of Wales were conquered in the thirteenth century. A number of the fortresses and fortified towns that were built to subdue the locals has been covered in our companion touring guide *Hammer Time: Travel and Travail with the Armies of Edward I*. Suffice it here to flag up that Beaumaris, Caernafon and Conwy, despite some local difficulties, are outstanding new towns and remarkable fortifications, built at great cost, and worthy of visiting in their own right.

There are one of two design flaws, such as a low wall at Caernafon facing the town, and Conwy not actually being finished, but don't let that put you off. Since these are covered elsewhere though, let's focus on a couple of the gateway settlements you may pass through in the south.

Monmouth is marginally over the border into the principality. There's a significant castle on the site, a favourite of the Dukes of Lancaster. It happens to be the birthplace of Henry V, making him a Welsh born Prince of Wales by geography if not by blood. The monastery is where the historian (we use that term loosely) Geoffrey of Monmouth was based. If you spot any pots cemented into the walls here or in any other monastery for that matter, don't try storing anything in them as they have been set into them to help with the acoustics.

Fortunately, being so far south east it manages to avoid most of the troubles arising from Glendower's Revolt. As you head west across the Monnow river, admire the bridge with its fortified gateway. We're seeing a lot of these disappearing over time.

Not much further into Wales you'll pass by Raglan. Late in the Low Season you'll find work begun here on a new great castle. Perhaps surprisingly, the castle is a building of many great windows, showering the insides with a surprising quantity of light. Especially remarkable is the huge bay window.

The Great Tower, surrounded by a mini moat, almost reminds you of a lighthouse, looking out onto the distant forbidding mountains but casting a protective pall around the parks, orchards and ponds that lie around.

The owner's a senior Welsh nobleman with experience in the wars, so you'll find plenty to talk about. Including why the gun emplacements have been sited so badly.

1453 and all that

Castillon - field of sorrow, shrubbery of despair.

All good things come to an end. The string of English successes is one of them. Your time to run rampant across the ramparts of the greatest power of Europe is finite.

The Hundred Years War leaves England weak and divided. France finally re-emerges united and strong. Was it a waste of gold and lives?

The end result is only part of the story. England's position at the outset was badly exposed, with the French monarch nibbling away at Gascony until nothing would be left. A series of brilliant victories and middling campaigns, backed by inventive use of the national debt and some lucky alliances, breaks French strength for a century, and delays the birth of a Greater Castile – the two great powers of the sixteenth century.

England too will rise again, though it will take thirty years of civil war to mend the monarchy first. There is perhaps a strange mirroring in that the Hundred Years War lasts pretty much the same length of time as the Tudor dynasty that will set this in motion.

But the era of great English empires in France is over. Old loyalties will fade. Once it finally succumbs, Bordeaux will have small garrison forts built in its heart to guarantee it will never revolt again. The castles are hated but make the point. The union with Paris is literally cemented. Within living memory of the fall, city leaders are commemorating the French King's triumphs in wars in Italy by building a victory gate leading onto the harbour.

The English and their doughty Gascons have a good run, but the French eventually find new tactics and mobilise their unstoppable strength. There is a symmetry in this, as the year of the fall marks the rise of two great powers at either end of Europe, each announced by thunder.

Two months separate the key dates that for historians close the medieval period. On 29 May 1453, Constantinople, the ancient capital of the dying Byzantine Empire and Rome's long-ailing successor, is stormed by the

Turks. On 17 July 1453, the battlefield of Castillon wrecks the last hope of restoring the old Angevin empire of the Kings of England. Cannon play a crucial role in both.

This truly is the end of old empires and the dawn of the kingdoms of gunpowder. A new age has begun.

And right now over in Germany, there's a new-fangled printing press to tell everyone about it.

Acknowledgements

The author would like to thank Frank Caldwell and Sandwell Council; Graham Sumner; Bury Council; Moya Watson and Cheshire Shared Services; Graham Smith, David Watkins and Michael Spender at Poole Museum; Gill Woolrich; Casper Johnson; Ben Croxford of Kent County Council; Gill Woolrich and Esta Mion-Jones at Southampton City Council; Moya Watson at Cheshire West and Chester Borough Council ; Tim Morgan; insert team at publishers

The photos are my own. Recent artwork is credited and acknowledged.

Further Study

This is not a definitive guide. This book is a taster and introduction, a field manual. With such a fascinating subject and range of players, we heartily encourage the reader to delve deeper.

Central to understanding the events of this period are three key chroniclers. Jean le Bel, Jean Froissart, and Enguerrand de Mostrelet between them cover the period, with natural bias and the very occasional error of detail, but also with a degree of collective thoroughness. This is the central and crucial port of call for first hand reporting. There are also a number of local chronicles providing regional flavour from this era. For entertainment value we thoroughly recommend tracking down the Byland histories; they slightly predate the period but are a lively insight to life, preoccupations and priorities.

A number of London City Livery companies, particularly the older ones that weren't bombed out during the war or incendiarised by the Great Fire, have interesting halls, and art and silver collections: see their respective websites for more details. The National Archives have an excellent website explaining some processes of government, as well as archival material online. The Royal Armouries are an excellent visual source.

Janet Hinson's translation of the French translation of the text of Le Menagier de Paris is happily online, providing direct and easy access to what is in large part a basic cookery guide from the fourteenth century. The online Catholic Encyclopedia is meanwhile a handy agglomeration of data on the history of the Catholic Church, including the occupants of Avignon, albeit written from a very particular viewpoint.

Students writing projects on narrow aspects of history might usefully check to see what JSTOR has to offer. This site provides a huge variety of academic articles and the chances are that amongst its archives there will be a couple that have some detailed and expert bearing on your project (such as finding out where malaria's northern limits ran to), or which at least can be used to sanity check interpretations of the primary source material. Similarly, http://www.british-history.ac.uk/ hosts an extremely useful selection of reports detailing individual buildings and their history. Sites that have been designated as Scheduled Monuments by English Heritage (or its equivalents) typically have a listing somewhere detailing the history and significance of a given site, which is extremely useful for local context.

However, those seeking an overview across the decades should as part of their journey head for the magisterial and brilliant series of (admittedly hefty) tomes on the conflict by Jonathan Sumption. They are embracing, academically thorough, and very agreeable to read. We are impatient to see the remaining promised volumes in print.

Finally, there is no replacement to visiting the castles, battlefields and buildings of the time themselves.

ALSO IN THIS SERIES...
The Discerning Barbarian's Guide to Roman Britain
The Discerning Gentleman's Guide to His Majesty's North American Colonies
The Discerning Tourist's Guide to the End of the World (coming soon)